The Right Letter!

The Right Letter!

How to Communicate Effectively in a Busy World

Jan Venolia

Author of *Write Right!*, *Rewrite Right!*, and *The Right Word!*

Ten Speed Press

BERKELEY • TORONTO

Originally published by Ten Speed Press as *Better Letters: A Handbook of Business
and Personal Correspondence*, © 1981, 1982, 1995 by Janet G. Venolia.

Ten Speed Press
Box 7123
Berkeley, California 94707
www.tenspeed.com

Distributed in Australia by Simon & Schuster Australia, in Canada by Ten Speed
Press Canada, in New Zealand by Southern Publishers Group, in South Africa by
Real Books, and in the United Kingdom and Europe by Airlift Book Company.

Cover design by Paul Kepple
Text design by Tasha Hall
Illustrations by Ellen Sasaki

"Ask Dr. Science" excerpt on page xv reprinted with permission from Ask Dr. Science,
2003, www.drscience.com.

"Snail Mail" on page 75 verse copyright © Indian Hill Press. All Rights Reserved.
Reprinted with permission.

Library of Congress Cataloging-in-Publication Data
   Venolia, Jan.
      The right letter! : how to communicate effectively in a busy world / Jan Venolia.
         p. cm.
      Rev. ed. of: Better letters. 2nd ed. c1995.
      Includes index.
      ISBN 1-58008-635-7
      1. Letter writing—Handbooks, manuals, etc. 2. English language—Rhetoric—
      Handbooks, manuals, etc. 3. Commercial correspondence—Handbooks,
      manuals, etc. 4. Interpersonal communication—Handbooks, manuals, etc.
      I. Venolia, Jan. Better letters. II. Title.
      PE1483.V4 2004
      808.6—dc22

                                             2004015746

Printed in Canada
First printing, this edition, 2004

1 2 3 4 5 6 7 8 9 10 — 09 08 07 06 05 04

To my amazing grandchildren,
Riley, Celeste, Analisa, and Marisela.

Write to your grandmother!

> *An odd thought strikes me: We shall
> receive no letters in the grave.*
> —Samuel Johnson
>
> *In the meantime . . .*
> —Jan Venolia

Contents

*Our correspondences have wings—
paper birds that fly from my house to
yours—flocks of ideas crisscrossing the
country. Once opened, a connection is
made. We are not alone in the world.
—Terry Tempest Williams*

Acknowledgments

There are some hazards associated with being one of my friends or a member of my family. At any given time, you might be asked to critique a manuscript, suggest suitable topics or examples of errors, devise goofy names, or be queried about pet peeves (such as common grammatical errors or email overload). Your conversation and correspondence might be mined for quotes or other usable bits.

It is a mark of true friendship and an indication of the strength of family ties that such help has not only been forthcoming but unstinting, plenteous, and accompanied by a generous dollop of good humor.

For this particular book, I give heartfelt thanks to the following stalwart souls:

Carrie, Skylar and Ward Anderson, Joyce Cass, Carmen Ramos Chandler, Al Chapman, Emily Copeland, Pat Ditzler, Marcia Dorst, Amir Hussain, Peggy Holloway, Mark Jackson, Peg Myers, Jay Thoman, and the core Venolias: Carol, Lee, Malcolm, and Wayne.

The editor responsible for weaving all the strands together has been Ten Speed's Kathryn Hashimoto, impresario extraordinaire. Thanks, Kathy!

Mail Call

Letters illuminate emotion, humanity, and
fortitude in a way that is always fresh
and enduring. They are the color,
heart, and personality of history.
—Dorie McCullough Lawson

Do people still write letters? With so many other ways to communicate, have letters been crowded out?

Not at all! Letters help people do important things: Land a job, make a sale, express thanks, send condolences, or simply keep in touch. Letters are less intrusive than the telephone, giving both writer and reader the luxury of a second look. You can't revise what's been said in a phone call, let alone remember exactly what was said.

The Right Letter! covers both business and personal correspondence, from cover letters for resumes to thank-you notes. The book also includes suggestions for improving your email style and for reducing the number of groans that email often provokes.

Because business letters usually affect your livelihood, most of the pages that follow are devoted to writing effective business letters and email. Personal letters, by their nature, will be written and read in a more relaxed way; nonetheless, if the help you're looking for is how to write a letter of sympathy, you'll find it here as well.

The Right Letter! does not cover such standardized forms of business communication as interoffice memos or fax cover sheets. Nor is it a manual of instructions for the email novice. It doesn't advise you about equipment, discuss the technical aspects of connecting to the Internet, or acquaint you with the joys and hazards of blogs and newsgroups. *The Right Letter!* does provide suggestions for improving your email style. By implementing these ideas, you might just find that you're helping make email more useful and enjoyable for everyone.

Is the message you send by email pretty much like the letter you send by snail mail? No. You toss off a casual email message with little or no revision, unconcerned whether it would make your English teacher beam—or wince. If you're applying for a job, however, that's clearly another matter. You need to give each kind of message its due. Start by sorting your communication along the following lines.

Use the **U.S. Postal Service** to send:

- job applications
- cover letters (e.g., accompanying a proposal)
- letters that are two or more pages long
- material concerning confidential matters
- letters that call for official signatures (such as contracts or letters of agreement)
- sympathy and personal thank-you letters

Use a **fax** for:

- sending a hard copy quickly
- providing customer support (e.g., instructions, parts lists)

Use **email** for:

- sending short, informal messages
- making group announcements

Use the **telephone** or **instant messaging**:

- when you need an immediate response
- if the subject requires discussion
- for the back-and-forth of brainstorming

Three out of four of these methods of communicating require that you know how to write. Unfortunately, people are increasingly unsure of how to choose and organize words—an uncertainty you may feel yourself. *The Right Letter!* will help you develop the skills and confidence you need to become a better letter-writer.

The Right Letter! is divided into three parts. In PART ONE, *Business Letters*, the basics of style and organization are presented in Chapter 1, "The Nuts and Bolts of Letter-Writing." Chapter 2, "The Look of the Letter," addresses matters of appearance: format, typeface, and placement of text on the page. Chapter 3, "Examples of Business Letters," translates matters of style, organization, and appearance into sample letters—not as templates for you to mimic, but as suggestions to stimulate your creative juices.

PART TWO, *Personal Letters*, covers the kinds of letters you are called upon to write as friend, consumer, and citizen.

Chapter 4, "The Joy of Personal Letters," touches on the areas where some advice might be needed in this more relaxed genre. Chapter 5, "Examples of Personal Letters," suggests how to write specific kinds of letters.

Part Three, *Email,* explores the love/hate relationship many of us have with email. In Chapter 6, "Avoiding Email Anarchy," I suggest some ways for you to cut back on the frustrations of this powerful medium while being a better email correspondent. Chapter 7, "Writing an Effective Email Message," presents a few solid rules for improving email style in an area where rules seem to change daily.

The Appendix provides some useful lists: abbreviations preferred by the U.S. Postal Service, as well as the most commonly used Internet domain names (both domestic and international). You'll also find the correct way to address a letter to your senator, someone in the military, a school superintendent, your CPA, or a parish priest.

With today's technology you can express mail a letter across the country in a day or email one around the globe in an instant. But writing an effective letter is still up to you. *The Right Letter!* can help you transform what might be a frustrating task into a rewarding endeavor.

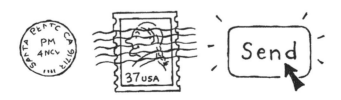

Dear Dr. Science,

I am 26 years old and can't remember what it was like to live without the Internet. Do you remember what it must have been like?—Jerry Roberti from Milwaukee, WI

Just barely. I'm 47, and my memories of a Webless World are as diaphanous as the seat of my old suit pants, but it seems to me that people used to read and write. They would hold pieces of paper in front of their faces and grunt softly in understanding, or sometimes imprint words on a piece of paper and then wrap that piece of paper in another, put a gummed picture of a dead person on it, and place the whole arrangement in a box, waiting for someone to physically take it across the country, or sometimes even the world, to its intended recipient. I know it sounds crazy, but the antiquated system used to work, most of the time. Now that system is only used to send bills and junk mail. But back in the olden days, that's all there was.

Part One
Business Letters

1 The Nuts and Bolts of Letter-Writing

> *Letters should be easy and natural, and convey to the persons to whom we send just what we would say if we were with them.* —Lord Chesterfield

Assume the person you're writing to is busy, that you have to compete for the recipient's attention. If your letter is written and presented well, you're ahead of the pack.

To be effective, your letters should be:

- NEAT. Make a good first impression; the opportunity doesn't come along twice.

- CLEAR. Help your reader understand your message and avoid misunderstandings and ambiguities.

- ACCURATE. Your reader should be confident that you are providing correct, precise information.

- PROMPT. Answer letters at the earliest opportunity; this will encourage your correspondent to do the same while helping you look responsible and interested.

- FRIENDLY. Stress "you" rather than "I"; show that you understand your reader's situation.

- BRIEF. Don't waste a busy person's time with excess words and redundancies.

- CORRECT. Use words properly; spell and hyphenate them correctly. Look up words you are uncertain about.

- COURTEOUS. Include courtesies such as "thank you" and "please" even in the briefest letter.

- COMPLETE. Don't leave loose ends; provide the necessary information in appropriate detail.

By following the guidelines above and throughout this chapter, you can write a letter that incorporates the elements of style in an organized and attractive manner. With practice, effective letter-writing will become second nature.

> *I have received no more than one or two letters in my life that were worth the postage.*—Henry David Thoreau

Style

Business letter-writing is a special kind of writing, directed toward a particular audience for a specific purpose. You may have an audience of one or of thousands. Whatever your objective, make your writing style clear, concise, and readable.

The stilted, flowery language that used to characterize business writing went out of style with ink wells and quill pens. Today, good business writing follows a few straightforward rules, expressing ideas clearly and succinctly.

Be clear.

Make it easy for your reader to understand why you're writing. Have your objective clearly in mind: I want to get a job, make a sale, establish goodwill, or any of the myriad reasons for sending a business letter. Then use the kinds of words that will help you succeed. Get rid of stale, vague, and weak words; replace them with fresh, specific, and strong ones.

Stale: If it meets with your approval . . .
Fresh: If you approve . . .

Vague: We experienced a marked increase in productivity after management introduced a program to improve employee health.
Specific: The exercise and nutrition program cut absenteeism in half.

Weak: A sharp drop occurred in the Dow Jones Industrial Average.
Strong: The Dow Jones Industrial Average dropped sharply.

> *The most useful and interesting letters we get here from home are from children seven or eight years old. . . . They write simply and naturally and without strain for effect. They tell all they know, and stop.*—Mark Twain

Be concise.

As you can see, the "better" examples above and on the preceding page are not only more vigorous but shorter as well. Don't waste a busy person's time with unnecessary words.

> *The most valuable of all talents is that of never using two words when one will do.*
> —Thomas Jefferson

Remove padding, leaving only words that are essential to your meaning. For example:

ROUNDABOUT	DIRECT
in view of the fact that	
owing to the fact that	because
due to the fact that	
some questions relating to this issue	some relevant questions

Delete empty phrases such as *consideration should be given to*, *you can appreciate that*, and *in this connection*. If possible, avoid clauses that begin with *there is* and *there are*.

> **Wordy:** There are several companies that are qualified to do the work.

> **Better:** Several companies are qualified to do the work.

Shorten and invigorate sentences by replacing forms of the verb *to be* (*is, am, are*) with action verbs.

> **Wordy:** The attached resume is indicative of my knowledge and experience in this area.

> **Better:** The attached resume indicates . . .

> *I have made this letter longer than usual, only because I have not had the time to make it shorter.*—Blaise Pascal

Wherever suitable, compress clauses beginning with *which, that,* or *who*.

> **Wordy:** The plan that we are proposing would take less than two weeks to implement.

> **Better:** The proposed plan takes less than two weeks to implement.

If you're tempted to prop up a word with an adjective or adverb, consider whether the word alone is stronger.

> **Poor:** Your vote in this matter is truly crucial.

> **Better:** Your vote in this matter is crucial.

Be readable.

In a world of automated tellers, customer service lines, and voice mail, the human touch is welcome. Add it to your letters by writing in a readable style.

Choose a suitable tone. Make the tone of your letter appropriate for the recipient and for your objective in writing. Obviously, a letter to someone you've never met (but you're hoping will hire you) will be more formal than a note to a friend in the hospital. An effective sales letter will be persuasive; the response to a complaint, conciliatory.

> Dear Sir (or Madame),
> You may be right.
> Sincerely yours,
> H. L. Mencken
>
> (Mencken purportedly printed these cards and mailed them in response to unread letters from angry readers.)

Write in the active voice. The active voice is forceful, direct, and often requires fewer words than the passive voice.

Passive: Your report was read by the committee.
Active: The committee read your report.

Passive: Revisions of the charter have been made to remove outdated provisions.
Active: We revised the charter to remove outdated provisions.

Emphasize important points. Give the reader visual clues (by using bullets, italics, and numbering, for example) to make important points stand out. But don't overdo such flourishes. Resist the temptation to italicize every word you want to stress, and don't overemphasize a word by making it both bold-face and underlined. A page cluttered with too many gimmicks dilutes its impact and distracts the reader.

When creating a bulleted or numbered list, make each item parallel in sentence structure.

Nonparallel:

1. I organized meetings and created agendas.

2. Assigning each group member a task was another of my responsibilities.

3. Progress reports were regularly issued by me.

Parallel:

1. Organized meetings and created agendas.

2. Assigned tasks to each group member.

3. Issued progress reports to the group.

Use paragraphing to help the reader. Group ideas and provide visual breaks with paragraphs. By arranging sentences in coherent units, you provide spacing that gives the page a more pleasing, readable appearance; this, in turn, makes your ideas more accessible.

Provide road signs for the reader. Use words and phrases to bring the reader along with you. For example, to signal the direction you are taking:

> To explain the concept briefly,
>
> Best of all,
>
> As I mentioned on the phone,

to indicate a change of course:

> However,
>
> Despite this,
>
> In contrast,
>
> On the other hand,

to stress important points:

> Here's the key to the whole program:
>
> Now, for the most exciting development,
>
> By acting now,

Such road signs increase the likelihood that both letter-writer and reader will arrive at the same destination.

Avoid sexist terms. For generations, masculine terms have been used to indicate both sexes. Today, however, many recipients will be offended if you start a letter with *Dear Sir*. Some will feel excluded if you write, "The effective salesman pays attention to his customers' needs."

Avoiding sexist terms is surprisingly easy. Here are a few suggestions to get you started.

- Replace *Dear Sir* with the Simplified Letter Format, which omits the salutation (see p. 32).

- Use gender-neutral words, such as *worker, service rep*, and *flight attendant*.

  Poor: The man who holds the chalk controls the meeting.

  Better: Whoever holds the chalk controls the meeting.

- Where appropriate, rewrite to avoid masculine pronouns. For example:

  Poor: The consumer can stretch disposable income if he refrains from impulse buying.

  Better: The consumer can stretch disposable income by refraining from impulse buying.

Be courteous. This is a point worth repeating: Saying *please* or *thank you* is always appropriate. Courtesy is an important characteristic of letters of all lengths.

Letters that are clear, concise, and readable will generally follow the rules presented in this chapter. But rules are only guides for most situations. You needn't *always* write with short words, brief sentences, and the active voice. If you know the rules, you can decide when it's suitable to break them. In doing so, you will be acting from knowledge, not ignorance.

You'll find more on the specifics of good writing in two of my other books: *Write Right!* and *Rewrite Right!*

Organization

Write for people who skim. Busy readers may do little more than check out the first and last paragraphs to see if anything interests them.

Arouse interest with your opening paragraph.

Your first paragraph is both the headline and the lead for the message that follows. Establish a favorable impression with direct, positive words.

> As soon as your letter arrived, we phoned your order to our St. Louis office.

> Your appointment as general manager is good news indeed.

> You are right in assuming we want to hear from our customers.

Avoid openings that restate the obvious:

> I have received your letter of October 16 . . .

have a negative tone:

> We cannot understand your failure to comply . . .

or use clichés:

> At Fletcher's, the customer is always right. So, better late than never . . .

Become a collector of interesting facts. If you keep a file of quotations, curious statistics, and stray bits of information, you may find ways to turn them into openings or weave them into the body of a letter.

I recently received a letter that opened with a compelling statistic:

> Enough food is produced in the world to meet the nutritional needs of every child, woman, and man. But every day, *34,000 young children die* from malnutrition and disease.

I had to read on. (The letter ultimately asked for a charitable contribution.)

Have you tried starting a sales letter with a question? Here's one that hooked me:

> What do tennis balls and our mailing lists have in common?

I wanted to know, so again, I read on. (The price of both is the same as it was ten years ago.) Here are some other opening questions:

> Do you want to avoid a tax audit?

> How long has it been since you've had some free time?

> Are you ready to trade in your commute for an office at home?

Another example from my files illustrates the hazards of a poorly worded question. The letter began,

> Do you like the idea of saving money and convenient equal monthly payments?

My reaction was that I especially liked the idea of saving those convenient equal monthly payments. Word your question carefully!

People enjoy a humorous quotation or tasteful anecdote:

> Years ago, Mark Twain offered some advice that's still on target for today's investor: "Put all your eggs in one basket— *and watch that basket!*"

> At Investors.org, we help you follow Twain's advice.

Humor can backfire, however. Use it with sensitivity to possible offense.

Make your letter the right length.

A letter should be just long enough to do the job. Say what you have to say—politely, clearly, and briefly. You show the greatest consideration for readers when you take only enough of their time to convey what is important.

The body of the letter can be one paragraph or longer, depending on the subject. Use separate paragraphs for different points, with a logical progression and clear transitions to guide the reader.

Leave a good impression with your closing paragraph.
The main function of the final paragraph is to bring your letter to a courteous, businesslike close. Where suitable, you want to be persuasive. A summary is appropriate only if your letter is long. When action is called for, indicate what you want the reader to do or what you will do. Use positive words: *when* not *if*.

> **Poor:** Call me if you want more information.
> **Better:** I will gladly provide more detailed information—just give me a call.

> **Poor:** I will try to call you next week to see if we can find a convenient time to get together.

> **Better:** I will call you next week to see when we can get together.

The amount of pressure you apply depends on the nature of the letter. A goodwill letter sent in order to maintain a friendly working relationship might end with a low-key closing:

> Let us hear from you when we can be of help.

You apply a little more pressure if you ask a question:

> May we send our technical representative, Gene Poole, to demonstrate our new desktop model?

Strongly urging a specific action is the high-pressure end of the spectrum. Readers should understand why they would want to comply.

> Use the enclosed information sheet to order your copies today. The books will be on their way to you promptly.

Just complete the enclosed questionnaire. By return mail we will send you a free 16-page booklet that's full of good advice on stretching your food budget.

Please send your check promptly to cover the overdue balance.

A weak ending diminishes the effectiveness of an otherwise well-written letter. Avoid the following:

Participial phrases

Thanking you in advance,

Hoping for a favorable reply,

An apologetic attitude

I'm sorry I haven't been of more help.

Clichés

At this point in time,

In the final analysis,

Last but not least,

Your reader carries away a favorable impression when you make the closing polite and to the point.

Final Steps

When you have completed a letter, pause and change hats from author to reader. Although routine correspondence may require nothing more than a careful proofing, if your letter is important (say, one going to thousands of customers or to one potential employer), it should be given a cooling-off period. Overnight, if possible. When you reread it, you want to see the letter as if for the first time.

Revise what you've written.

Review your letter, asking questions such as the following:

- Have I made my point(s)?

- Have I used too many words?

- Do the sentences and ideas flow smoothly?

- Have I avoided stilted language and redundancy?

- Is the emphasis where I want it to be?

- Was I in a bad mood ˙ wrote the letter?

As you develop good habi letter-writing becomes easier. Your short letters may need little or no revising, but long or important ones should always be revised. You can invariably make them more readable. See *Rewrite Right!* for more detailed suggestions for improving your writing.

Proof carefully.

Skimping here can undo all your efforts to make a good impression. Reread not only for typos, but for omitted or incorrect words.

> When you have said something, make sure you have said it. The chances of your having said it are only fair.—E. B. White

Unfortunately, you are most likely to miss errors in precisely the places readers are most likely to notice them—namely, in the first lines of a paragraph, page, section, or heading. Take extra care at every beginning.

Following are some proofing techniques I've found helpful:

Use a ruler or straightedge. Place the ruler just below the line you're reading; this reduces the chance you'll skip anything.

Read the letter aloud. Awkward phrases and grammatical glitches are more evident when you *hear* them.

Read it backwards, from bottom to top, from right to left. This way, your eye doesn't slide past repeated words, since you aren't reading for meaning.

Use a dictionary or spell-checker. Correct spelling is a hallmark of the careful, educated writer. One wrong letter or a simple transposition turns *gather* into *father*, *marital* into *martial*.

As you undoubtedly know, a spell-checker has shortcomings. It's up to you to catch omitted or wrong words or mix-ups of homonyms such as *there* and *their*. For example, can you spot the error below?

> Look for prescription drugs on which the patients have expired.

I hope the correct word is *patents*, not *patients*!

When you've found one error, look for others nearby. Mistakes often come in clusters. Ironically, this may be the result of revising. When you make a change, you may fail to notice that you've left behind stray words or phrases. Clean up after yourself.

Look for double trouble. Is every opening parenthesis followed by a closing parenthesis? Do quotation marks come in pairs?

There's no safety in numbers. Errors in numbers can be catastrophic, so proof any numbers in your letter especially carefully. Also check whether you've mixed up units of measure: inches and centimeters, miles and kilometers, dollars and pounds.

Double-check line and page breaks. Have any words been repeated or omitted?

Check the spelling of names. Recipients may barely register that you spell their name correctly, but they *always* notice if you spell it wrong.

As you develop the skills you need for an effective business letter, all of your writing will benefit—from the hastily dashed-off email to the carefully crafted proposal. Your sales letters will be persuasive, your proposals convincing. And your job application? Hey, it will help you land that job!

2 The Look of the Letter

> Then there's the joy of getting your desk clean, and knowing that all your letters are answered, and you can see the wood on it again.—Lady Bird Johnson

It takes more effort to read a carelessly put-together letter than one that is orderly. If your letter is neat, well placed on the page, and pleasing to the eye, you're off to a good start.

Composing your letter on a word processor can help. If your software includes a template with a typeface and layout that you like, use it. If you prefer, you can easily create your own combination of fonts and spacing.

For most correspondence choose one of the standard typefaces (for example, Times Roman or Courier) in 12-point type. Unusual fonts such as *Script* or Comic are a distraction and are harder to read. Use a ragged-right alignment of the text for easy reading. Right-justified alignment has the appearance of pages in a book rather than a letter; it can also result in irregular spacing within lines. Choose a neutral-colored stationery, and set your printer for the highest print quality.

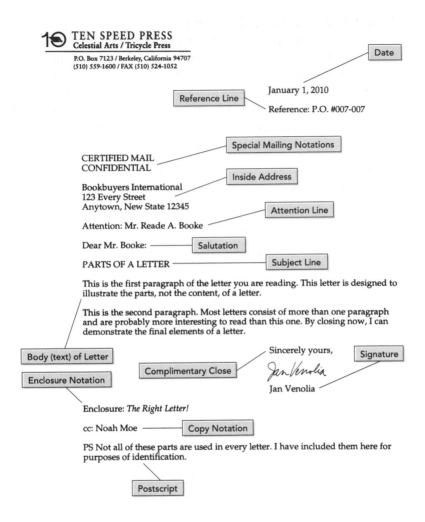

TEN SPEED PRESS
Celestial Arts / Tricycle Press

P.O. Box 7123 / Berkeley, California 94707
(510) 559-1600 / FAX (510) 524-1052

Date

January 1, 2010

Reference Line

Reference: P.O. #007-007

Special Mailing Notations

CERTIFIED MAIL
CONFIDENTIAL

Inside Address

Bookbuyers International
123 Every Street
Anytown, New State 12345

Attention Line

Attention: Mr. Reade A. Booke

Dear Mr. Booke: Salutation

PARTS OF A LETTER   Subject Line

This is the first paragraph of the letter you are reading. This letter is designed to illustrate the parts, not the content, of a letter.

This is the second paragraph. Most letters consist of more than one paragraph and are probably more interesting to read than this one. By closing now, I can demonstrate the final elements of a letter.

Sincerely yours,   Signature

Body (text) of Letter

Complimentary Close

Jan Venolia

Enclosure Notation

Jan Venolia

Enclosure: *The Right Letter!*

cc: Noah Moe   Copy Notation

PS Not all of these parts are used in every letter. I have included them here for purposes of identification.

Postscript

Letter Placement and Design

A pleasing layout that helps the reader concentrate on the substance of your letter follows a few simple principles. Think of a letter as a picture, with the margins serving as its frame. Set the left and right margins according to the length of the letter: 1 inch for long letters (300 or more words, two or more pages), 1¹/₂ inches for average-length letters (100–300 words), and 2 inches for short letters (fewer than 100 words).

A short letter placed high on the page looks as if the writer ran out of things to say, while a long letter with the signature block squeezed onto the bottom of the page suggests poor planning.

To make a short letter fill the page, increase the space between the parts of the letter: date and inside (recipient's) address, inside address and salutation, and complimentary close and signature block. Use space-and-a-half line spacing for very short letters (two or three sentences).

To make a long letter less crowded, edit the text to make it shorter or start an additional page; carry over at least three lines of text to the continuation page. Set the margins of continuation pages to match the first page; include the date, name of addressee, and page number at the top.

Some of your choices depend on whether you use preprinted stationery or plain paper. The important thing to remember is that the look of the letter says something about you, so be sure to take a moment to assess its appearance before sending it out.

LETTER PLACEMENT

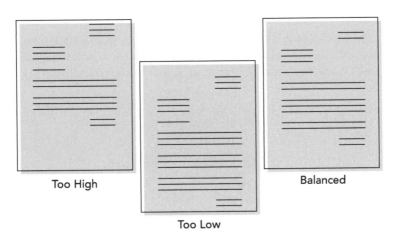

Too High

Too Low

Balanced

Letter Formats

Minor variations in layout (with or without paragraph indentations, for example) used to have complicated nomenclature (Modified Semiblock, for instance). Now the terminology and choices are more straightforward.

Do you want the ease of having all parts of the letter (date, address, close) begin at the left margin? If so, use the Block Format. Do you prefer a more balanced appearance? Then use the Balanced Format, which places date and closing on the right-hand side of the page.

Do you want to avoid using a salutation, because you aren't sure if the recipient is Mr., Ms., or Mrs.? The memo-like Simplified Letter is your choice. Any of these formats (Block, Balanced, or Simplified) is acceptable and easily implemented.

The following guidelines assume that you will be using letterhead of some kind (either preprinted stationery or letterhead you've created within the document). If you're not using something preprinted, you need to decide what contact information to include: your mailing address, telephone and fax numbers, email address, and perhaps a website. Place this information about an inch from the top of the page flush with the left margin (for Block and Simplified) or flush right or centered (for Balanced).

The Block Letter

The Block Format has the virtue of being easy to use, which to many of its advocates outweighs its lower score for aesthetics. The Block Format seems to fit today's high-speed society.

- Begin all lines at the left margin.

- Place the date two to six lines below the letterhead.

- Place reference line flush with the left margin, two to four lines below the date.

- Place the inside address two to six lines below the date or reference line.

- Place the salutation two to four lines below the inside address.

- If a subject line is used, capitalize it and place it two lines below the salutation.

- Begin the body (text) of the letter two lines below the salutation or subject line.

- Do not indent paragraphs.

- Place the complimentary close two lines below the last line of the body of your letter.

- Place the signature block four lines below the complimentary close.

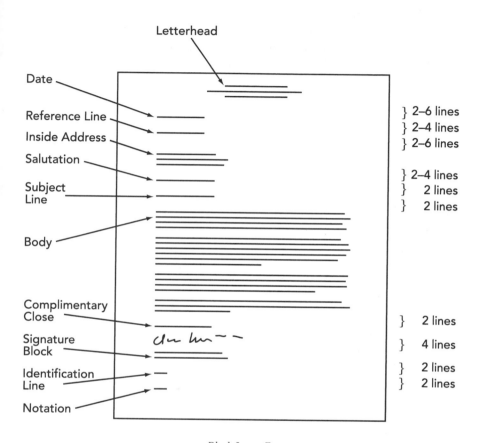

Letterhead

Date

Reference Line — } 2–6 lines

Inside Address — } 2–4 lines

Salutation — } 2–6 lines

Subject
Line — } 2–4 lines
} 2 lines
} 2 lines

Body

Complimentary
Close — } 2 lines

Signature
Block — } 4 lines

Identification
Line — } 2 lines

Notation — } 2 lines

Block Letter Format

The Balanced Letter

Those who are attuned to the aesthetics of the page prefer the Balanced Format because it's more, well, balanced.

- Place the date two to six lines below the letterhead, so that it ends at the right margin or begins about five spaces to the right of center.

- Place reference line two to four lines below the date.

- Begin the inside address at the left margin, two to six lines below the date or reference line.

- Place the salutation at the left margin, two lines below the inside address.

- Begin body of letter two lines below salutation or subject line. Do not indent paragraphs.

- Align the complimentary close and signature block with the date; leave two lines between the body of the letter and the close, and four or five lines between the close and the signature block.

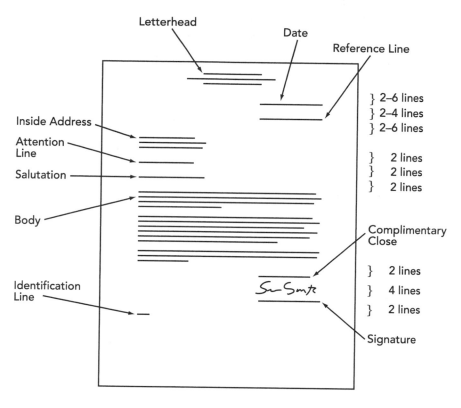

Balanced Letter Format

The Simplified Letter

The Simplified Letter solves the *Dear Sir* problem by eliminating the salutation. However, if you know the recipient's name and gender, it's better to use one of the traditional, more friendly formats that includes a salutation and complimentary close (the Block or Balanced Letter).

- Do not use a salutation.

- Begin all lines at the left margin.

- Place the date two to six lines below the letterhead.

- Place the inside address three or four lines below the date.

- Type the subject in caps, three lines below the inside address and above the body of the letter; do not use the words *Subject* or *Re*.

- Begin the body (text) of the letter three lines below the subject line.

- Do not use a complimentary close.

- Type the letter-writer's name and title, in caps, four or five lines below the body of the letter.

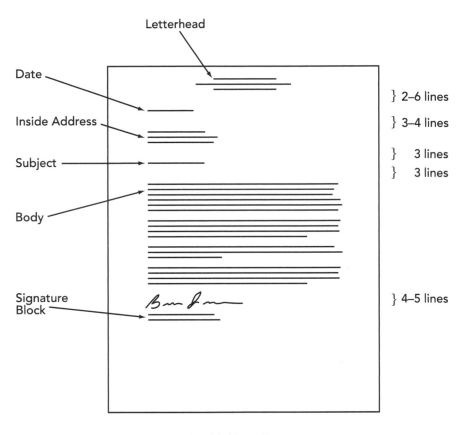

Simplified Letter Format

The Elements of a Letter

The formats described in the preceding paragraphs cover placement on the page of the various elements of a letter. Let's now look at some of the elements themselves.

Date

Don't abbreviate (Nov. 1) or use numbers (11/5/15). If you prefer, the standard order of month and day (November 25, 2010) may be reversed and the comma omitted (25 November 2010). This style is customary in the U.S. government, in the military, and in countries outside of the United States. Whichever style you choose, be consistent throughout the letter. Place the date two to six lines below the letterhead.

Reference Line

If the content of your letter can be easily identified by a reference (for example, an invoice or purchase order number), place it two to four lines below and lined up with the date. Some prefer to place the reference line where the attention or subject lines would appear in a letter, which is also acceptable.

Special Mailing Notation

To indicate special circumstances involving delivery or handling on arrival, place the notation flush left between the date and inside address.

If both method of delivery and on-arrival notation are used, place the special-mailing notation first (for example, *by registered mail, fax,* or *overnight delivery*) and the on-arrival notation underneath (for example, *Personal* or *Confidential*).

Inside Address and Salutation

A courtesy title (*Mr.*, *Dr.*, *Ms.*, *Mrs.*) precedes the name of the addressee, and, where applicable, a professional title follows the addressee's last name. (See the Appendix for more on professional titles and forms of address.)

Dr. Kara Lott, Chief of Staff

Mr. Landon Bridges, CPA

Place long professional titles on the second line of the address.

Ms. Iona Carr
Vice President and General Manager

Omit the courtesy title if the name is followed by *Esq.* or by the abbreviation for a degree.

N. R. Childe, MD

Terry A. Weil, Esq.

When addressing more than one individual, place the names on separate lines in alphabetical order (by last name), not "ladies first" order.

Mr. Harold Angell
Ms. Sarah Fimm

Dear Mr. Angell and Ms. Fimm:

When addressing a couple where one or both are titled, you have additional choices. When both have a title:

Drs. Dodie and Earl E. Byrd
or Drs. Earl E. and Dodie Byrd
or Dr. Dodie Byrd and Dr. Earl E. Byrd

Rev. Pearl E. Gates and Dr. Ames Hyer
or Dr. Ames Hyer and Rev. Pearl E. Gates

When only one has a title:

Dr. Carrie Wood and Mr. Sylvan Wood

The Honorable I. C. Kohn and Ms. Mardi Graw

Col. Todd L. Long and Mrs. Beryl A. Long

Whenever it is known, use the form preferred by the individuals you are addressing. People are usually sensitive about their names and will notice if you get it right—or wrong.

If you know the name but not the gender of the recipient, you can use the Simplified Letter, which omits the salutation (see p. 32), or you could use the addressee's full name:

Dear Robin Banks:

The salutations *Dear Sir* or *Gentlemen* are an unacceptable solution when you don't know your addressee's name. *Dear Sir or Madam* and *To Whom It May Concern*, though more even-handed, have the musty aura of a bygone era. The following are better choices:

Generic Titles: Certain categories of addressees lend themselves to the grouping of a generic title:

Dear Homeowner: Dear Parents:

Dear Employee: Dear Customer:

Job titles or company names are sometimes used:

Dear Credit Manager:

Dear Editor:

Dear Ten Speed Press:

Dear General Motors:

Generalized Salutation: You can occasionally use the casual *Hello* or the even more casual *Howdy!*, but you're probably on safer ground with one of the salutations above or with the salutation-free Simplified Letter (see p. 32).

Attention Line

Use an attention line when your letter is addressed to a company or organization in general but you wish to bring it to the attention of a specific individual. Place the attention line flush with the left margin, two lines below the last line of the inside address. Do not abbreviate the word *Attention*; a colon following the word is optional.

Subject Line

The subject line identifies the content of the letter in a few well-chosen words. It is part of the body of the letter and thus is placed two lines below the salutation, either centered or flush left. In the Simplified Letter, which has no salutation, the subject line is placed flush left, three lines below the last line of the inside address.

It can appear on the line by itself in all caps (Simplified Letter) or be underlined and introduced by *Subject:* or *Re:* (Block or Balanced Letter).

Body (Text) of the Letter

Begin the text of your message three lines below the subject line in the Simplified Letter and two lines below the salutation or subject line in Block or Balanced formats. Use single-space for most letters, with double-space between paragraphs. If a letter is very short, you may use space-and-a-half or double-space. Indent or center special material within the body of a letter, for example, numbered or bulleted lists; single-space within each item, and double-space between items. Set off long quoted material from the rest of the letter by indenting it from both left and right margins.

In general, avoid abbreviating words in the text of a letter; exceptions are social or professional titles (*Dr.*, *Mrs.*) or words that are usually abbreviated, such as company names (*Intl.*, *Ltd.*). Abbreviating other words gives the impression that you are too rushed or uninterested to be more careful. I once received a letter from a department store addressing me as *Dear Cust.* The space and time saved by not typing the remaining four letters were a poor bargain for the store.

Letters of More Than One Page: Use printed letterhead only for the first page of a letter. Type continuation pages on plain sheets that match the letterhead stationery or on printed second sheets. Carry over at least three lines of text to any continuation pages, and make the margins the same as on the first page.

Type the heading for second sheets six lines below the top of the page, flush left, and include the addressee's name (if the letter is addressed to two individuals, each name appears on its own line), the page number, and the date. Leave four or five lines between the heading and the text of the letter on continuation sheets.

Complimentary Close

Place the complimentary close two lines below the body of the letter, either at the left margin (Block Letter) or aligned with the date (Balanced Letter). It should not extend beyond the right margin established by the body of the letter.

Capitalize only the first letter of the first word of a complimentary close; end it with a comma.

Highly formal:

Respectfully,

Respectfully yours,

Polite, formal (general correspondence):

Very truly yours,

Yours truly,

Friendly, less formal (general correspondence):

Sincerely,

Sincerely yours,

Yours sincerely,

With best regards,

Informal, friendly (when writer and recipient are on a first-name basis):

As ever,

Best regards,

Best wishes,

Regards,

Signature

The signature block is aligned with, and four or five lines below, the complimentary close. It consists of the writer's name in the form preferred by the writer (e.g., G. V. *Train*, *Gray V. Train*) and the writer's title. If a title is used, it is placed on the same line as the name or one line below it.

G. V. Train, President

Gray V. Train
Vice President and General Manager

In the Simplified Letter, the writer's name is typed all in caps, flush with the left margin, four or five lines below the body of the letter.

If letterhead stationery is used, do not include the company name in the signature block; if letterhead is not used, type the company name in caps two lines below the complimentary close, and the writer's name (only initial letters capitalized) four lines below the company name.

If the letter deals with personal matters, omit the writer's title. The department name, business title, and writer's name may be omitted if they appear in the letterhead.

When two people sign a letter, place the names on the same line, with the first name flush with the left margin. If there isn't room for both names on one line, place the second name four spaces below the first signature block.

If you are signing a letter for the writer, place your initials just below and to the right of the signature.

Identification Line

An optional identification line can be included to show the initials (lowercase) of the person who is typing the letter; it may also be preceded by the initials (uppercase) of the sender, in which case both sets of initials may be separated by a colon or slash. It is usually typed flush left, two lines below the signature block.

Enclosure Notation

Enclosure notations serve both as a check to the letter recipient that everything was actually enclosed and as a reminder to the letter-writer of what was sent. *Enc.* or *Enclosure(s)* is typed flush left, two lines below the signature block.

Copy Notation

If you wish the recipient to know who is receiving copies of the letter, type *cc:* and the name of the individual(s) flush left, two lines below all other notations (that is, after the signature line and the enclosure notation).

Postscript

A postscript is typed flush left, two to four lines below the last notation. The initials *PS* preceding the text are optional. Use postscripts sparingly. You don't want to give the reader the impression that you are unorganized or indecisive. But since they do catch the reader's eye, postscripts can be used effectively. Here's a humorous example, written by Mark Twain to Andrew Carnegie:

Dear Sir and Friend:

You seem to be in prosperity. Could you lend an admirer $1.50 to buy a hymn-book with? God will bless you. I feel it; I know it. So will I.

Yours, Mark

PS Don't send the hymn-book; send the money; I want to make the selection myself.

Envelopes

Your main concern about envelopes is meeting the requirements of the U.S. Postal Service, such as placement of both the recipient's and sender's names and addresses on the front of the envelope, the size of font (address should be legible from an arm's length away), and so on. Word-processing software for addresses takes care of this; you can also obtain the information at the postal service website (www.usps.com). There you'll find a complete list of zip codes, information on how to wrap packages—even how to apply for a post office job.

> *The postman is the agent of impolite surprises. Every week we ought to have an hour for receiving letters—and then go and take a bath.*—Friedrich Nietzsche

3 Examples of Business Letters

Some books about letter-writing consist entirely of sample letters. Just find the one that comes closest to what you want to say and fill in the blanks. The results are predictable: a letter lacking any spark of originality.

My goal in *The Right Letter!* is to help you create one-of-a-kind letters, not a one-size-fits-all letter. The letters included here are designed to stimulate your own ideas about writing to a prospective employer, customer, or colleague. Think of it as my teaching you how to fish instead of handing you a trout.

A business letter represents you and your company. Your written words will influence the reader's opinion about your business savvy and strengths. With that in mind, all business letters should be regarded as sales letters, though their immediate function may be as a cover letter, job application, or letter of recommendation.

When You're Looking for a Job

The letter you send hoping to get a job reveals a great deal about you. It tells potential employers you are well organized, thorough, and careful—or that you are sloppy, careless, and unwilling to take the time to do a good job. When your letter is read, you will not be there to add missing information or correct false impressions; for the moment, the words you put on the page represent you. Make them work for you.

A Word of Advice: Use stationery with your own contact information (home and email addresses, telephone and fax numbers), rather than the letterhead of your current employer. Though you may have been given permission to look for a job elsewhere during office hours, prospective employers may wonder if you would look for a job on their time, too. Some hiring officers feel so strongly about this that they won't interview applicants who use the stationery, email, or fax of their current employers.

Resume Cover Letter

Always send a cover letter when you submit a resume—it's what will make all the effort you put into crafting the resume pay off. A well-written cover letter enhances your resume in several ways: It allows you to provide highlights or details not listed in the resume, to target your approach to a specific company, to demonstrate your writing and communication skills, and to present a more personal and human side to your potential employer.

To write a successful resume cover letter, begin by clarifying your thinking. What do you want? What do you have to offer? Describe your accomplishments with action verbs; show results, not a laundry list of job functions. For example:

> Achieved 55 percent capture rate on proposals to business and government clients.

> Inaugurated and directed a marketing contact scheme that doubled our list of active customers.

Your letter must be error-free. No misspelled words, no punctuation errors, no incorrect usage. Be sure to deliver on any promise you make (for example, "I will phone next week.").

The following suggestions draw upon advice found in *The Damn Good Resume Guide* by Yana Parker (Ten Speed Press, 2002).

1. Address someone in authority by name and title. Be sure to spell the name correctly.

2. Mention how you became attracted to this particular company.

3. Demonstrate that you see the company's point of view (their problems, interests, priorities).

4. Convey your enthusiasm for this line of work.

5. Balance professionalism with personal warmth and friendliness. Avoid the stilted language often found in business letters.

6. Describe at least one distinguishable and relevant thing about yourself (for example, a talent for getting along with all kinds of people).

7. Be appropriate to the field you're exploring; stand out but in a nongimmicky way.

8. Identify both what you are seeking and what you are offering.

9. Tell what you will do to follow through.

10. Be brief and focused.

The Ineffective Cover Letter

Sometimes it helps to know not only what works but what doesn't work. In their book *Dynamic Cover Letters* (Ten Speed Press, 2001), Katharine and Randall Hansen list a dozen common qualities that can keep a cover letter from attracting the right kind of attention. Their points are abstracted here; see the Hansens' book for further discussion and illustration.

An ineffective cover letter has the following shortcomings:

1. A boring and formulaic opening paragraph.

2. Lengthy, uninteresting paragraphs, or a total length of more than one page.

3. An autobiographical tone rather than a sales pitch that would make the employer want to set up an interview.

---

4. Phrases such as "I think" or "I feel," which dilute the letter's effectiveness.

5. An unsolicited salary request.

6. Unnecessary negative information.

7. A desperate tone.

8. Ignorance of the company.

Job Application Letter

Occasionally, a letter substitutes for a resume. You might send it in response to a known opening, or you might be on a fishing expedition. The goal is to obtain that all-important interview.

About 500 pieces of paper cross the desk of a busy executive each week, so you have only a few seconds to grab someone's attention. Include just enough information to arouse interest in your qualifications.

Mr. Tom E. Hawke, Manager
Personnel Department
MegaCity Manufacturing, Inc.
1550 Industrial Parkway
Cleveland, OH 45555

Dear Mr. Hawke:

Roland Holmes told me of the job opening in your Marketing Department. I would bring initiative and enthusiasm to such a position.

In my ten years in sales, I have demonstrated an unusual ability to find new markets and to develop novel applications for existing products. For example:

- I developed the market for a line of books to be featured in quick-print shops, which led to nationwide distribution through print-shop franchises.
- I supervised the design and staffing of a trade show booth that doubled our usual number of sales leads.

I'm confident that my background matches the qualifications you are seeking. Could we meet to talk about it? I will phone next week.

Very truly yours,

May K. Diehl

Ms. Tanya Hyde, Director
Human Resources Department
KOOL-TV
Public Broadcasting Towers
Washington, DC 20000

Dear Ms. Hyde:

Strong public-interest programming makes KOOL stand out among D.C. television stations. My experience at the Ivy College Clarion and radio station K-DUDE make me an exceptional candidate for your summer intern program.

The individuals on the enclosed list of references are familiar with both my academic record and my work at the D.C. Youth Center.

Working at KOOL has long been my dream. I hope your intern program will be the first step in turning that dream into reality.

Sincerely yours,

Cal Stanford

If you have limited job experience, or none at all, consider what you *do* have to offer a potential employer. With a little imagination you may find it's just what an employer needs. For example:

Dr. Mal D. Mayer
Medical Mall, Suite 5F
356 Appletree Street
Madison, WI 56789

Dear Dr. Mayer:

Personnel turnover is often a problem in medical offices. That's why you will be interested in my background in hospital record-keeping—and my tenacity.

I have worked more than 5,000 hours as a volunteer at Harbor Hospital. My responsibilities included bookkeeping for the hospital gift shop (paying suppliers, recording sales, and transferring profits monthly to the hospital) and sorting about 300 pieces of patient mail each week.

I have a working knowledge of the forms required by insurance companies and by Medicare, based on assistance rendered to my elderly parents and to a number of their friends.

My interest in working in a doctor's office has prompted me to study medical terminology on my own. If your employee screening includes testing in this area, you will find that I have pursued my studies well.

I would be pleased to meet with you to discuss how I could provide the kind of help you are seeking. My phone number is 406-0298.

Sincerely yours,

Laurel Ann Hardy

When our son was looking for that hard-to-find first job, he sent the following letter to prospective employers:

If you are looking for summer help this year, please consider hiring me. It won't cost you much money, since my rates are low. But I will do a good job for you, because I am quick to learn and eager to please.

I have some mailroom experience, a California driver's license, and I'm six feet tall, so I can reach high places. I could perform errands, clerical duties, odd jobs, or library research, to name a few possibilities.

My abilities are indicated by a 3.5 grade point average (I'm a senior at City High School, graduating in June) and by my earning a general ham radio license when I was 15. I would really like to turn those capabilities into experience.

He got the job.

Letter to Request a Reference or Recommendation

The terms *reference* and *recommendation* are often used interchangeably in the context of job seeking. Perhaps the best way to differentiate between them is to say that writing a letter of recommendation is an explicitly enthusiastic show of support, while providing a reference can either be a positive review or a more neutral confirmation of employment details.

Usually, you are asked to provide the names of three or more references, either personal or professional, who can vouch for the attributes, qualifications, and experience you claim in your application, or to provide further, illuminating information about you. The references may be in the form of a list of names and contact information or as letters that you have already obtained.

It's important to contact your potential references ahead of time to make sure they are willing to provide support, either by writing a letter or making a phone call. Your request accomplishes three things:

1. The person has the opportunity to say no if he or she does not wish to participate.

2. You can prepare the person by describing your current situation, the job you're seeking, and what type of information might be requested by the potential employer.

3. You can remind the person of specific details, situations, and positive qualities that could help your cause, particularly if some time has elapsed since you last saw the person.

The strength of your references can make the difference between getting and not getting a job, so be sure to select references carefully and make it as easy as possible for them to help you. Also, remember to be courteous and appreciative of the person's voluntary time and support.

Ms. Polly Graff
Polygraphics PR
101 Main Street, Suite 5-B
Seattle, WA 98000

Dear Ms. Graff:

I am applying for the position of Publicity Director at Peters Publishing. Would you be willing to be a reference for the years I worked under your supervision at Polygraphics?

As you may recall, I was hired as a trainee in public relations, following my graduation from Ivy College. My early assignments emphasized writing press releases and developing multimedia aspects of our clients' public relations programs. I also served informally as the in-house person to call if there were problems with the Zappo Multimedia 9.9 System.

I left Polygraphics five years ago, to gain experience in developing client accounts; the enclosed resume fills you in on some details of those years.

The opening at Peters appears tailor-made for my background in public relations and my interest in publishing. I would be grateful for your help as a reference. Please let me know if you need further information.

Thank you.

Sincerely,

Anna Graham

Post-Interview Thank-You Letter

A follow-up letter after an interview makes you stand out as thoughtful, businesslike, and interested in the job. Don't fall into the trap of thinking that you can skip this step. A thank-you letter—even if it's a short, handwritten one—may be the best way to make you stand out from the other candidates.

Ms. Roxanne Stones, President
ADVENTURE Clothing Design
Central Tower, 10th Floor
Denver, CO 80200

Dear Ms. Stones:

When I visited ADVENTURE headquarters yesterday, I was impressed by the exceptional workplace environment you have created. I had read of your company's innovative approach to management-employee relations, but it was exciting to see it in action.

The visit confirmed my belief that my years as a buyer of women's clothing at Brandhoff's Department Stores would be an asset for ADVENTURE. I hope you agree.

Thank you for taking time in your busy schedule to meet with me.

Sincerely yours,

Hope Springs

Send your letter to the person who interviewed you (be sure to spell his or her name correctly), and refer to the date of the interview and the position desired. Underscore any strong features of the interview, your responses to new information about the job or company that came from the interview, and your updated view of how you could fit into the company.

When You're on the Job

With every letter you write on the job, you are representing your company. View it as an opportunity to present your company in a good light.

Cover Letter

A cover letter may be one or two sentences that serve only to identify what is enclosed (for example, a brochure, booklet, report, sample, or proposal). Or you may wish to pique the recipient's interest in a full page that highlights or expands on the enclosure.

A sloppily written cover letter sabotages your purpose—a point illustrated by the letter I once received from an insurance agent. In the span of two short paragraphs, he left out an important word, repeated himself unnecessarily, and failed to notice that the closing *Sincerely* appeared twice! Although the agent presumably wanted my business, his sloppiness with a routine letter made me wonder if he was as careless when handling claims. Avoid sending such mixed messages. (See pp. 46–49 for a discussion of cover letters that accompany a resume.)

The cost of heating or cooling a home is a significant part of the household budget. Inflation and higher energy prices have forced homeowners to choose their heating and cooling equipment with care.

The enclosed booklet describes state-of-the-art systems that you can install today. It compares the energy efficiencies of various models and indicates how soon each would pay back your investment.

This brochure is part of Consolidated MegaPower's ongoing commitment to keeping customers informed about energy-related matters. We welcome your comments or questions.

Sales Letter

Marketing programs often rely on letters to acquaint potential buyers with their products. The effective sales letter focuses on the appeal of the product or service to a particular market:

- Saving (spending less)

- Profit (getting more)

- Health (preserving or improving it)

- Comfort (enjoying a feeling of well-being)

- Convenience (saving time, increasing efficiency)

- Prestige (having pride of ownership, keeping up with the Joneses)

- Enjoyment (experiencing happiness, personal satisfaction)

The following letters respond to several of these motivations.

DOWNTOWN GYM OPENS

Have you ever noticed that people who survive a heart attack suddenly start watching their diet and getting more exercise? There's a reason: Their bodies have just sent them a powerful message.

A heart attack is a compelling way to get your attention, but it's also a risky one. It's smart to get the message without the heart attack. And the message is clear. Regular exercise and a sound diet improve the quality and length of our lives. We all know it, but many of us put off doing anything about it.

The new Downtown Gym can change that. Our extended hours and convenient location allow you to schedule exercise breaks at any time of the day or evening.

What does Downtown offer? State-of-the-art equipment, swimming pool, Jacuzzi, sauna, and handball courts. Our staff of personal trainers teaches regularly scheduled classes and is on hand for one-on-one sessions. Dr. Eaton Wright consults with members about losing weight and planning healthy menus.

The enclosed brochure describes our facilities and the various types of membership. Drop in and give us a try during February, when we're offering a free trial week. You'll be doing your heart a favor.

DINA SAWYER
VICE PRESIDENT, MEMBERSHIP

Dear Mr. and Mrs. Aiken-Hart:

Insurance is a gamble . . . between you and the insurance company. But there's one thing that's a sure bet: You're paying too much.

At ABC Financial Services, we tailor an insurance program to your situation, whatever your income or financial goals. Our plan not only covers all the important elements—emergency funds, inflation, retirement, and disability or death—but it adds up to less than you're paying today.

Call me at 665-0000 for more information or to schedule an appointment. I'd be happy to meet at any time that's convenient for you.

Let us help you keep the lid on the cost of living.

Sincerely yours,

Penny Wise

Business Thank-you Letter

In business, as in personal matters, expressions of appreciation are always welcome. Even a short note of thanks maintains and strengthens relations. Develop the habit of writing thank-you notes: It's one of the best ways to apply your letter-writing skills.

Lacey Valentine
Valentine Management LLP
1567 Peachtree Towers
Atlanta, GA 34567

Dear Lacey:

Thank you for yesterday's thought-provoking seminar. You showed that you're well acquainted with the challenges of a consulting business.

We have already started to implement several of your ideas about flexible hours and plan to phase in the more ambitious child-care program in the months ahead. Then we'll invite you back to assess our progress and inspire us once again.

Sincerely,

Forrest Greene

Letter of Reference or Recommendation

When you write a letter of recommendation for a friend, colleague, or employee, include such information as the following:

- length of time you've known the individual

- nature of your acquaintance or relationship (e.g., supervisor, classmate)

- your evaluation of the individual's qualifications in general, as well as for the particular job (if known)

When writing, keep in mind that unless the individual has signed a waiver forgoing the right to see your letter, it may one day be read by the person it describes. The amount of detail will reveal your level of enthusiasm. A few generalized statements suggest a satisfactory performance; paragraphs of detailed description indicate superior qualifications.

If you are asked to write a professional reference or recommendation, you may want to check first with a human resources administrator in your company before complying. Some companies have a policy, for legal or security reasons, regarding the type of information that can be provided in such a letter. In some cases, information may be limited to verifying dates of employment, job title, and job description.

Dr. Lindsay Woolsey
Graduate Admissions
University of the World
Mail Drop B-25
Collegeville, UT 87654

Dear Dr. Woolsey:

Rose Gardner has worked under my supervision for the past five years. Her assignments concerning the geophysics and chemistry of manganese nodules called for a grasp of fundamental principles as well as meticulous attention to detail. She proved to be industrious and skillful in carrying out assignments.

> Ms. Gardner developed software that helped us convert raw data into useful form; she calibrated our sedimentometer and used it to measure systems of interest. Her experience with instrumentation includes the DigiMax B-2000 ultracentrifuge and the Ellery 21 spectrophotometer.
>
> Ms. Gardner brings to her work a high degree of integrity. Her intellectual vigor and tenacity suggest that she is well qualified to enter your PhD program.
>
> Very truly yours,
>
> Manuel Schiff, PhD

Form Letters

In businesses with a lot of routine correspondence (for example, an insurance agency, a fundraising firm, a literary agency), form letters are time-savers. Once you have the wording needed for one situation (such as filing an insurance claim, acknowledging a financial contribution, or responding to an author), it can be used repeatedly. Your goal in creating a form letter is to make it look individually written—which is remarkably easy with a word processor.

Once you have established frequently used letters as templates, you can individualize them by inserting specific information. Add some flourishes—the individual's name inserted in the text, a handwritten *Thank you* in the margin—and the letter will give no hint of its assembly-line origin.

Letter template:

> Dear _____:
>
> Please use the enclosed form to describe the incident that occurred at your home on _____,
> that resulted in _____.
> Include any details that would help explain_____
> _____.
>
> We will process your claim as soon as we receive the completed form. I enclose a self-addressed, stamped envelope for your convenience.

Completed form letter:

> Dear Mr. and Mrs. Sippi:
>
> Please use the enclosed form to describe the incident that occurred at your home on January 1, 2010, that resulted in the hospitalization of three guests. Include any details that would help explain how they came to be on the roof.
>
> We will process your claim as soon as we receive the completed form. I enclose a self-addressed, stamped envelope for your convenience.

Letter of Resignation

Accepting a position with another company, job dissatisfaction, and retirement may call for a letter of resignation. Often such a letter documents an event that has been expected or discussed by all parties. A single sentence may suffice:

Please accept my resignation, effective November 1, 2015.

You may also want to include information or express sentiments beyond such a bare-bones statement. Let your intention determine the tone and content.

Make your letter friendly if you wish to maintain strong ties with the company you are leaving. Even if your aim is to document grievances, an objective tone is advisable.

Ms. Helena Basquette, District Attorney
Broward County
One Courthouse Square
Miami, FL 33333

Dear Ms. Basquette:

In the eight years I have served as prosecutor, I've worked hard to obtain convictions, despite an ever-diminishing budget for investigative support.

It is with regret that I conclude I can no longer do the job I was hired to do. With this letter I am resigning my position as Deputy District Attorney, effective immediately.

Very truly yours,

Jay L. Warden

Letter of Regret

Occasions arise that call for a letter declining an opportunity—perhaps a job offer, a speaking engagement, or acting as a reference. The letter can be brief, but still maintain goodwill.

Here's a letter Guglielmo Marconi, inventor of the radio, might have written in 1912 when he had a change of plans.*

Mr. Don E. Brooke, Chairman
White Star Steamship Company
Liverpool, England

Dear Mr. Brooke:

I regret that I must cancel your thoughtful arrangements for me and my family. We would have enjoyed being on the maiden voyage of "the engineering marvel of the century." However, circumstances have forced a change of plans.

Though we will not be on board, our spirits will be with the *Titanic* when she sails from Liverpool next week.

With my sincere thanks,

Guglielmo Marconi

---

*Note: Though the letter is imaginary, the circumstances were not. Gavin Weightman, author of *Signor Marconi's Magic Box*, describes the sadness Bea Marconi and her daughter, Degna, felt as they "waved to the hundreds of lucky passengers who leaned on the rail of the upper decks of the *Titanic* as the great liner eased out of Southampton Water on 10 April 1912."

Part Two
Personal Letters

The Joy of Personal Letters

> There is something very sensual
> about a letter. The physical contact of pen to
> paper, the time set aside to focus thoughts,
> the folding of the paper into the envelope,
> licking it closed, addressing it, a chosen
> stamp, and then the release of the letter to
> the mailbox—all are acts of tenderness.
> —Terry Tempest Williams

Think what a lift you get when you see a letter from a friend or relative in the stack of bills and junk mail. Yet even though we all like to receive those letters, few of us take the time to write them. It's a loss now and for future generations.

Letters are a time capsule of sorts. I've often been impressed upon reading a copy of a letter I'd written years earlier that I'd forgotten virtually everything in my letter—even though I wrote it. By having kept a copy, I was able to laugh again at a funny episode or relive a special moment. Letters help you get more mileage out of life.

> *That so few of us write to our children any longer, that we so rarely write personal letters of any sort, is a shame. I think often of how little we will leave about ourselves and our time in our own words. Maybe some of the e-mail will survive, but I doubt it. How will future generations ever come to know us?*—David McCullough

Perhaps you resist writing because you're not comfortable putting words on paper. With a little practice, though, you can overcome such feelings and make your letters the best way to keep in touch. If a friend experiences a death in the family or is seriously ill, a letter is one of the most meaningful ways to show that you care.

Sharing happy occasions is equally important: the excitement of travel, the fun of a class reunion, the joy of becoming a grandparent. The bonds we maintain through letters are a haven in our increasingly impersonal world.

> *One of the pleasures of reading old letters is the knowledge that they need no answer.*
> —Lord Byron

When Dorie McCullough Lawson, author of *Posterity: Letters of Great Americans to their Children*, asked for copies of letters Milton Friedman had written to his children, Friedman responded that he and his wife had "been able to communicate with them more directly by . . . telephone calls and the like so that we have no systematic collection of letters. Sorry." To which Lawson added, "Sorry indeed are we all, and future generations may be sorrier still."

Among my most treasured letters are those written by my father to his three daughters at the time we were born. A generation later he wrote welcoming letters to each of his grandchildren—a tradition I have continued with my own children and grandchildren. Such letters are all the more valued because they express emotions we don't often manage to communicate in person.

Handwritten or Typed?

Letters to newspaper editors to express an opinion or to companies to register a complaint will probably produce the best results if they are typed. The most personal of letters, such as those extending sympathy, congratulations, or thanks, should always be handwritten.

Whether you type or hand-write a keeping-in-touch kind of letter is up to you. Years ago, a typewritten personal letter would have been considered a social blunder. Today, it's the norm and carries no stigma. Writing a letter by hand is usually more time-consuming than typing, so friends and family receive more news in less of your time if you write at your keyboard.

However, if your mood is more suited to curling up with a pad and pen than staring at a monitor, then by all means write by hand. The more you enjoy the process, the better your letter will be.

> It's rough to say to people with a lot of nifty and expensive equipment, but there are still times when the only proper manner of communication is putting ink on paper.
> —Judith Martin ("Miss Manners")

The list of letters that Miss Manners insists must be handwritten includes those of thanks, condolence, the love letter, and the apology. She gives extra credit for a letter of "thanks for past or long-term deeds, such as bringing one up, being a valued friend or neighbor, or teaching one in the second grade." Such letters are "not strictly required, but they are all the more treasured."

> SNAIL MAIL
> E-mail rushes to and fro
> Since paper letters seem too slow,
> But we prefer the status quo;
> This card was sent by escargot.
> —Dan Waters

Style and Format

In contrast with business letters, personal letters do not have to compete for the recipient's attention. In fact, your letter may well be eagerly plucked out of the stack of incoming mail and read first. That doesn't mean anything goes, however. You will increase your recipient's pleasure at hearing from you if you observe a few do's and don'ts.

> *I consider it a good rule for letter-writing to leave unmentioned what the recipient already knows, and instead tell him something new.*—Sigmund Freud

Don't begin your letter with an apology for not writing sooner. It's a common trap to fall into. Even if your letter is overdue, why waste everyone's time on the obvious fact that you haven't written—unless the reason for failing to do so is amusing or of special interest (like a trip to Hawaii or having won the lottery).

Sorry I haven't written   I have so much to tell you!

If you establish a file for letters written and received, you can keep track of what you or your correspondent last wrote about. This allows you to pick up the thread at that point and avoid repetition.

The format of personal letters is simple. Put the date near the top of the page, usually on the right side. Don't include your address, unless you're using a personal letterhead or have recently moved. Place a comma or exclamation point following the salutation, instead of the colon used in business letters.

Dear Samantha, or *Hi, Jonathan!* or just the individual's first name is a good way to begin.

If your letter is handwritten, indent paragraphs about an inch; if typed, double-space between paragraphs rather than indenting. If possible, avoid dividing words at the end of lines. Place the complimentary close and your signature slightly to the right of center. That's about all there is to it.

> *The reason I dread writing letters is because I am so apt to get to slinging wisdom and forget to let up. Thus much precious time is lost.*—Mark Twain

5 Examples of Personal Letters

> Letter writing is the only device for
> combining solitude with good company.
> —Lord Byron

When you receive a letter from a friend or relative, notice what you like best about it. Those are the parts you want to emulate in your own letters.

As a Friend or Family Member

The following letters might be ones you are called upon to write. The examples I include suggest the spirit of the letters, not formulas that you must follow. Your own thoughts provide the key ingredient: sincerity.

> Write no matter how tired you are, no matter
> how inconvenient it is.—Theodore Roosevelt,
> who followed his own advice, penning
> 150,000 letters in his lifetime.

Sympathy Letter

For many, the most difficult letters to write are those expressing sympathy. People often fear their words will be inadequate and may hesitate to write. As a result, the person experiencing grief may be cut off from much-needed support. When you reach out, you show that you care.

A personal note is more meaningful than a purchased card. By writing a couple of sentences, you can convey your sympathy.

Letter 1:

The news of your loss has saddened us both. We send you our sympathy at this difficult time.

Letter 2:

It was with sadness that I learned of your wife's death. Please accept my sincere condolences.

Letter 3:

While no word of mine can ease your loss, I want you to know that you are in my thoughts at this time of sorrow.

If you are a close friend or member of the family, sharing your remembrances and feelings can be a comfort. Anecdotes that reveal the person's character help keep alive the memory of the loved one.

Michael's death came as a tragic shock. Few seemed more full of life than he, making the loss all the more keenly felt by us all. Mike was one of the most mature young men I have known. He

always knew how to put everyone at ease and could usually find something to laugh about—including his own mistakes.

This period of grieving will be difficult for you. We miss Michael too, but he is very much alive in the memory of all who knew him. Our thoughts and prayers are with you.

When death comes in later years, you can mention the long, full life of the person; when an infant or child dies, the untimely loss.

Letters of sympathy reflect the character and beliefs of the person writing them. Obviously, you should not use the occasion to try to convert the recipient to a particular point of view, but you should feel free to express yourself in religious terms if those are the words that come to you naturally. Divergence of religious beliefs is unimportant when the desire to console is sincere.

Response to a Sympathy Letter

A brief note in response to expressions of sympathy is appropriate.

Letter 1:

Thank you for being so thoughtful. Letters such as yours have meant a great deal to me at this time.

Letter 2:

Your memories of my father were a source of joy. Thank you for sharing them with me.

Thank-You Letter

Personal thank-you letters are a good idea any time you have been the beneficiary of someone's hospitality, generosity, or willingness to help. A commercial thank-you card is an oxymoron: It says you're appreciative—but not enough to write a letter.

Write the letter promptly; your sincerity is diminished if you allow a long interval to elapse.

Dear Celeste and Riley,

My visit to Chicago was a memorable occasion, made all the more so by your thoughtful hospitality. You certainly know how to make a guest feel at home!

The delicious meals were a treat, and the way you adapted to my irregular schedule helped me get more done than I had imagined possible.

Thank you for being such thoughtful hosts. I hope you'll plan on staying with me if your travels bring you to New England.

Cordially,

Marisela

When you receive a gift, even if you are not particularly thrilled with it, a brief note is in order. If you keep in mind that the gift was sent with the best of intentions, you can probably find something suitable to say.

Dear Aunt Harriet,

What a conversation piece the door knocker is! We are especially pleased to have this memento of your travels in India and appreciate your effort in bringing it back.

Many thanks.

Thank-you letters needn't be the exclusive domain of adults. It's smart (difficult, but smart) to encourage children to write thank-you notes. If you start early, you have a better chance of establishing a lifelong habit.

The main ingredients for a young person's thank-you note are similar to those for an adult.

- Be timely (write within a few weeks of receiving a gift); a thank-you should never be so late that it looks more like a reminder of an upcoming birthday than a thank-you for a gift already received.

- Mention the usefulness or suitability of the gift ("I really wanted that action figure you sent—you should see my collection now!")

- Provide some personal or family news, or perhaps a recollection of being together ("The other day I thought about the cookies we made last time you were here. Can we make them again?"

- Say "Thank you!"

Letters from Parents to Children . . . and Vice Versa

Over the centuries, parents have used letters to advise their children: Study hard, resist temptations, make us proud, avoid bad companions—and write home!

A letter is usually welcomed when the child is away from home or no longer lives there, but not if it becomes a lecture in longhand.

> *[Parents] exhort and they sympathize. They caution, upbraid, tease, joke, teach, preach. They take pride and they take offense. And, of course, they offer no end of advice.*—David McCullough

The family dog gave both Groucho Marx and Frederick Law Olmsted a way to avoid the stereotype of the stern parent. When Marx wrote to his son Arthur during World War II, he assumed the voice of their dog, Duke. Duke's entertaining view of life on the homefront included reporting on the antics of his owners (Arthur's parents) and Duke's courtship of a collie in the 500 block of Palm Drive.

Olmsted (designer of New York City's Central Park) was asked by his four-year-old son Henry to send the family dog, Quiz, to Plymouth, where Henry was spending the summer. Olmsted responded with an imaginative excursion into life in New

York without Quiz there to chase six cats out of the yard every day: By the end of a week, there would be 42 cats, and in a month 180 . . . and so on. Of course, the cats would have kittens, and the imaginary heap (5,000 cats!) grew so tall that it blocked the light coming into Olmsted's office. If he couldn't see to do his work or couldn't sleep at night because of the racket the cats and kittens made (especially those on the bottom of the heap), he couldn't earn any money. If he couldn't earn any money, he couldn't buy his ticket to Plymouth at the end of the summer nor pay for Henry's ticket home—and they would never see each other again. Clearly Quiz had to stay in New York. What a delightful way to say No!

Your letters can best do the job of holding a family together if you use them to share your thoughts and show your affection. Be on the lookout for amusing incidents or local gossip to include.

Dear Leslie,

Yesterday I bumped into your friend Tim Burr at the gas station. He and his brother Lum are already home from college, but they will soon be leaving for their summer jobs. You will be green with envy when you hear what they'll be doing: smoke jumping! They are excited at such a bold departure from their usual summer jobs of slinging hamburgers, as you can imagine. But I must admit I don't envy their parents, who have an anxious summer ahead of them.

Steven performed at his annual piano recital last week. You will be impressed by how much he has learned since you last heard him play. No more "Starlight Waltz" for him—he's now into the three B's: Bach, Beethoven, and Brubeck.

We're counting the days till you're back home for the summer. Good luck with exams!

Love from us all,

Letters needn't be only from parents to children. What a radical idea! When distance separates family members, the arrivals of letters from children to their parents are welcome events. Even a brief note helps bridge the distance.

A letter is less intrusive than a phone call, which often seems to arrive in the middle of a meal. Letters can be read when it's convenient to do so; they can be savored and reread.

Dear Folks,

Let's see if I can get this note written in one swoop, instead of the usual segments over several days. Jonathan is napping, and Brittany is at a friend's, so a moment of quiet has settled over the house.

I thought the best indicator of life around here would be to tell you what happened this morning. When I opened the refrigerator, I found Brittany's sneakers on the shelf, snuggled right up next to the milk carton. No wonder I hadn't been able to find them!

I take some comfort from a friend's tale. She told me that when her kids were about the same ages as ours, she staggered into the kitchen one morning after a long night of crying baby to find her two-year-old asleep in the high chair. At least I haven't misplaced any of the children—so far.

Despite this glimpse of the occasional chaos here, we're managing remarkably well. And as is typical of succeeding generations, I find myself admiring more and more the job you did in raising me and my brothers.

Thanks—and love,

The Christmas Letter

An annual letter summing up the year may be the main way you keep in touch with family and friends. It deserves some care.

The art of the Christmas letter lies in knowing not only what to include, but what to leave out. Here are a few suggestions:

- Describe big events—a new job, graduation, birth of children or grandchildren, being in the Rose Parade—but not your whole calendar

- Include a vignette from a trip rather than an extensive itinerary

- Report major health-related developments but not a detailed medical report

Notice what you like about the letters you enjoy receiving, the ones you keep when the holidays are over. Let them inspire you.

As a Consumer and Citizen

You have the power to influence corporations and government officials. One of the best ways to exercise that influence is to write letters. Today, the individually written letter is more powerful than ever because, alas, so few people write them.

Your letter will be most effective if you direct it to a specific individual. Checking with the reference librarian at your local library or a little sleuthing on the Internet can help with names and addresses.

Complaint Letter

Consumer attitudes and satisfaction are carefully monitored by most companies. If you have cause for complaint—sloppy workmanship, unsatisfactory service, or objectionable advertising policies—speak up! It can be to your advantage at many

Dear Acme Brake Company:
Last week I brought my truck in to you for a complete overhaul...

levels. When I wrote to a regional bakery to report that a loaf of their bread had given new meaning to "stone-ground flour," I not only received an apology but a fistful of coupons. And there wasn't a bit of stone in any of the free bread.

If you think your complaint deserves a wide audience, send copies of your letter to an appropriate agency: the Food and Drug Administration, Federal Trade Commission, or Better Business Bureau, for example. Knowing some officials are hearing from you might put a little fire under the feet of the offending company.

> *If you want to make a corporation nervous,*
> *put something serious about it in writing.*
> *—Jamie Court, in Corporateering:*
> *How Corporate Power Steals Your Freedom*
> *. . . and What You Can Do About It*

Outline your case before you start writing; facts and emotions often become tangled if you don't first sort them out. Unless you make it clear why you are angry—even boiling mad—you may not get the desired result. Assume that the reader is intelligent and wants to hear your views.

November 30, 2010

Morgan County District Court
837 East Fourth Avenue
Wilsonville, IN 45678

SUMMONS D29783584

I do not deny that I was driving above the speed limit on River Road on November 3, 2010. I accept the fact that I needed a reprimand. I would like, however, to request that the court consider lowering the amount of my fine.

At ten miles per hour above the posted speed limit, I believe that I was driving safely, given the road and traffic conditions. Evidently the driver of the car ahead of me thought so, too, as he was traveling even faster than I was (and didn't get ticketed!). Under the circumstances, I think the fine of $150 is excessive. Please consider whether the punishment fits the crime.

Thank you.

Cliff Hanger

Occasionally a tongue-in-cheek approach works.

Dear Computer:

I've never written to a computer before, but it seemed the only option left to me. You and I are locked in an unending dance, the steps of which are roughly as follows:

(1) You write (6/15/20) stating that charges to my account at Brandhoff's have exceeded the allowed limit. You request payment of the entire balance plus penalty by July 1, 2020.

(2) I respond (6/20/20) pointing out that my April payment of $598 was never credited to my account—hence, the problem. I request that you check your records again and offer to provide a copy of my canceled check.

(3) Repeat of step 1. Letter slightly more urgent. Late charges pile up.

(4) I respond (9/21/20) by sending a copy of both sides of my cancelled check.

(5) Repeat of step 1. Letter threatens legal action.

Having failed to correct the situation with steps 2 and 4, I am appealing to you directly (step 6). I have taken all the necessary actions to confirm my timely payment and hope my appeal convinces you (or some live human being in Accounts Payable) to correct the situation.

Most sincerely,
Kent A. Ford

Fundraising Letter

Organizations and schools often take to the mail to raise money for their continued existence. If you are called on to write such a letter, make it as convincing and interesting as you can. You have a lot of competition in the mailbox, so it takes a careful choice of words—and maybe even a sense of humor—to make your letter effective.

Circumstances will determine the nature and content of your solicitation letter, and the target audience will determine how detailed your letter should be. In general, a positive, friendly tone will have good results.

Keep in mind that your goal is a difficult one: getting people to part with their money! One effective approach is to personalize the action by indicating what a given donation will buy. For example, five dollars buys a book for the Village Tutoring Center; one hundred dollars vaccinates a hundred children against polio for life; and so on. Also, you can help make things easier for the potential contributor by including a return envelope or postcard (with postage prepaid, if possible) with your letter.

Dear Friend,

How about a fund-raiser where we don't ask you to:

- buy or sell raffle tickets
- bake cookies
- make phone calls
- run a 10K race
- serve on a committee
- clean up afterward

In this community, where we are often asked to donate our time and energy to raise money for worthy causes, we thought the direct approach would be a refreshing change. So we're skipping the time-and-energy part and just asking for your money!

The worthy cause in this case is our local schools. Shrinking budgets have taken their toll on classroom activities, eliminating programs that most of us agree are important educational tools. The Foundation for Local Education (FLE) was established to address these needs. Each year, teachers and school volunteers apply for FLE mini-grants of up to $500 for equipment or activities.

The scope of their ideas is dazzling: from mastering mathematics to hands-on art projects, from stream rehabilitation to multicultural studies. What they are able to achieve with those grants is what FLE is all about.

Please join us in funding this investment in the future. We are all stakeholders in the education of our students.

Thank you.

Communicating with Elected Officials

What's the best way to communicate with an elected official? That's the question I recently asked interns in the offices of my representatives in Washington, D.C.

Is a letter sent through the mail more effective than an email? Is a faxed letter as good as a standard letter? Is a phone call better than any of these? The responses confirmed my suspicion that, at least in this case, *how* you communicate doesn't matter. What matters is that you *do* it.

Each intern had a different preference: One liked phone calls, another faxes, and the third thought a standard letter is best.

They all said an email gets as much attention as any other method of communicating, though none mentioned it as their first choice.

Where I found unanimity among the interns was in the importance of providing a typed or printed version of your name when you send a letter. "You wouldn't believe some of the signatures I've had to decipher," one commented. Making their job easier in this way is a good idea.

Here's what happens when you communicate—by whatever means—with your elected official. The intern translates your message into a tally: *For* or *Against* a given policy or piece of legislation. Your deathless prose, your well-reasoned argument, becomes a slash mark on a scorecard that tracks public sentiment. This suggests that one sentence clearly stating your position will save everyone's time. Such a sentence might be "Please vote against the Energy Bill," or "Please vote for SB106."

Well, make that two sentences. It's always nice to say *Thank you!* as well. Representatives in government also like to hear from you when you approve of their position or actions. If you want to encourage them to continue in a certain direction, let them know you appreciated their vote. A thank-you, in the sea of demands and complaints, is like a breath of fresh air.

Letter to the Editor
Here's the place for your deathless prose and well-reasoned arguments (see previous section). Think of a letter to the editor as your soapbox in Hyde Park, London's colorful venue for anyone with a strong opinion and a sturdy pair of lungs. It's an opportunity to exercise your freedom of expression.

You stand the best chance of convincing some of the undecideds of the merits of a given viewpoint if you present the reasoning behind it in a few concise sentences. If possible, cite authorities who agree with your position and can add a quotable point. Resist name-calling or belittling others whose letters appeared earlier, if your letter is written in response.

Dear Editor:

The term "global warming" is an unfortunate choice of words. It sounds a little like a day at the beach. Even the term "greenhouse gases" sounds friendly; I mean, greenhouse—that's where plants grow, right? The terms don't begin to suggest the droughts, fires, floods, and species extinctions that are already happening as a result of the increase in the earth's temperature.

Global warming may also fall into the too-big-for-me-to-worry-about category. A leaky faucet or those extra pounds I put on recently—now, *those* are things I can do something about. The irony is that leaky faucets and surplus weight will be utterly insignificant if we don't do something about global warming.

Global warming is not a natural cycle like an ice age. It isn't just our bad luck to be here when global warming began. Rather, global warming is the direct result of human activity. Today we human beings use as much oil in six weeks as we did in a whole year in 1950.

According to Bill McKibben, author of *The End of Nature,* "New ways of behaving, of getting and spending, can still change the future." The steps to take are available now, not just on the drawing boards. We need to pressure the politicians (who *do* pay attention if enough of us shout loud enough), and we need to reexamine our own "getting and spending." Let's change old ways of behaving as if our lives depend on it—which they do.

Part Three
Email

6 Avoiding Email Anarchy

> *. . . like a phone call only written . . . like a*
> *paperless letter, but faster. It's like a casual*
> *conversation, or a postcard, or a scribbled*
> *note to a schoolmate in the middle*
> *of class*—Jacque Leslie

Here's a little test to try on your friends: Ask how they feel about email. I predict their first response will be a groan.

Everyone's in-box is jammed. The daily need to slog through dozens, sometimes hundreds, of messages is daunting; returning from vacation can be a nightmare. Add a big serving of spam, incomprehensible acronyms, and sloppily compiled electronic mailing lists, and it's easy to see why we're suffering from email indigestion.

> *Everybody has about a 40 percent immediate*
> *cull rate—those pieces of mail you can delete*
> *immediately. . . . What you read of the*
> *remaining 60 percent depends on how much*
> *of a life you have. The less of a life, the more*
> *mail you read.*—Douglas Coupland

Rx for Email Heartburn

Clearly, some corrective actions are needed, but what can you do? Start by installing filters and exercising "unsubscribe" and "please remove" options to reduce the unwanted email. Then demonstrate by your own actions the kinds of standards you wish were in place. Proof outgoing messages, use carefully targeted mailing lists, and be courteous. In short, be a role model!

Many uses of email are beyond the scope of this book. Forwarding jokes, circulating political news, and participating in discussion groups are all part of making email a lively medium, but they require no comment from me. Instead, I focus in the following paragraphs on subjects where you might find a few suggestions helpful.

Who should receive your email message?

The biggest pet peeve among those I interviewed for this book was the listserv* run amok. Messages of no interest or pertinence—often from someone within one's own organization—can be more annoying than spam. A typical example: Notice of a luncheon meeting hundreds of miles away when there is no likelihood the recipient will attend. If everyone receiving the notice responds by clicking "Reply All," the insult is compounded.

Make sure your distribution list is accurate. If you routinely send messages to people with no interest in the subject, you're saying: "I'm too busy to decide who should receive this. You figure it out." After a while, recipients might not bother to open anything with your name on it. The phenomenon of crying wolf comes to mind.

In a similar vein, if your response to an email message doesn't concern everyone else who received the message, don't add to the clutter by clicking "Reply All." Respond just to the sender.

To ensure that replies sent to a mailing list come back only to you, address the message to yourself and send it to everyone else as a "bcc" (blind carbon copy).

> Email reflects a yearning to trade in the formality of writing for the spontaneity of speech.—Jacque Leslie

*Note: The capitalized term LISTSERV is the registered trademark name of a company selling software to manage electronic mailing lists. The lowercase spelling (listserv) is widely used as the generic term for such lists.

When should you use email?

Short, informal messages—both business and personal, local and overseas—are the best uses of email. The email format also lends itself well to in-house memos:

> The company cafeteria will be closed for remodeling next week.

> Blanche White's retirement party will be Friday at 4:30.

and to announcements that may be of interest to many:

> Page Turner will be the featured speaker at the Feb. 1st mystery-writing seminar.

> It's a girl!

When should you avoid email?

If you want to brainstorm a subject, email can be a terrible waste of time. In-person meetings, instant messaging, or conference calls are more efficient—and productive—ways to communicate interactively.

Always hand-write personal messages. Email is not a suitable way to send a letter of condolence or a personal thank-you.

> *Email has made it too easy for people to express every fleeting thought.*
> —Tom Tomorrow

Avoid sending email when you are angry or upset. Words sent in haste can't be recalled after you've calmed down. Sarcastic remarks can be misunderstood when stripped of the accompanying gestures or voice inflections.

> *I doubt that many people print out their email, tie it with a ribbon, and save it in a trunk in the attic.*—Roger Simon

Attachments

Attachments typify how email can be an ideal solution in some circumstances and a nightmare scenario in others. Here are a few things to consider when sending attachments:

Opening Attachments

"I couldn't open it" may be an occasional response when you send an attachment. Incompatible software—or even limited computer skills—can make opening an attachment difficult for some of your recipients. In those instances, cut-and-paste the material into the body of the message, or use snail mail.

Printing Long Documents

Who should print long documents, you or the recipient? Screens are harder to read than printed pages, so many people print long documents in order to be able to read them more comfortably. If shifting the burden of printing to your recipient is inappropriate, print and mail it yourself. A good example would be an unsolicited manuscript. You won't win points with a potential publisher by sending it as an attachment.

Virus Concerns

The fact that hackers often transmit viruses via attachments makes some people uneasy about opening them. Your intended recipient may need your reassurance in a separate email or phone call that the attachment is virus-free.

If you can navigate your way through all those difficulties—incompatible equipment, printing responsibility, and viruses—attachments are a good way to send such documents as minutes of meetings, drafts of manuscripts or proposals, and copies of speeches or articles.

> ### VIRUS VERSA
> *The ongoing hazard*
> *Of catching a virus,*
> *Presents us with dangers*
> *That always require us*
> *To be on our toes*
> *Even though it may tire us.*
>
> *If we pick up a bug*
> *And our systems all crash,*
> *Our hard work and records—*
> *They're gone in a flash!*
>
> *To ponder this problem*
> *Soon makes me admirous*
> *Of primitive days*
> *With quill pens and papyrus.*

The Big Brother Factor

Confidentiality is an increasingly important consideration in the world of email. I'm not talking about the boss catching you using email for personal matters, though you should be aware of that possibility, too. I'm referring to weightier matters.

Computer files are subject to subpoena, as a glance at today's headlines will tell you. Current law school curriculum includes learning how to access email records. Did you realize that we now have computer forensics specialists? The job title alone sends a chill through me. You should assume that someone qualified in this field can access *your entire hard drive*. If you wouldn't want something to be made public, don't put it in an email.

7 Writing an Effective Email Message

> . . . a whole new fractured language—
> definitely not as elegant or polished as
> English used to be, but in a way, much
> more vital.—Jon Katz

Rules for email usage are a little like lines drawn in the sand. What's frowned on one day becomes mainstream the next. But rules based on reader comprehension and common courtesy are practical and durable. You should be as concerned about being understood and being considerate as you are about being speedy.

> Letter writing is generally a thoughtful art
> and typing email often is not.
> —Dorie McCullough Lawson

Some Commonsense Rules

The following rules have staying power. They will improve your email style while helping you be a responsible email citizen.

Respond promptly.

Though not always possible, a prompt reply may take less time in the long run than procrastinating. The postponed response doesn't go away, it just adds to the backlog, making you consider—again and again—"Do I have time for this today?"

Use the subject line.

There are several good reasons for entering a subject in the subject line with every message.

- Without a subject, many email programs cannot sort and prioritize the message.

- It might be rejected by spam filters.

- It's just plain annoying.

If possible, set your software to warn you if you've omitted the subject.

In general, treat the subject line of your email as just what it says: the place where you indicate your subject. It's your first chance to capture attention and an opportunity to reduce virus anxiety.

The subject line is not a good place to begin your first sentence. Though some people find ways to do this in casual messages without creating confusion, many recipients find the practice annoying. Keep your subject in the subject line and start your message in the body of the text.

Make your subject line accurate:

Agenda for 4/1 Meeting

I'm moving! Here's my new address

Concert Committee Update

Proposal Draft

When a good friend sends a message with the subject "The Best Birthday Gift I've Ever Had" or our accountant's subject is "Taxes," I know I'm interested. But when someone messes up my name while trying to give the impression of being a friend ("Janet G., I've been trying to reach you"), I send it—unopened—to the Trash (you may know it as the Recycle Bin on your computer).

Avoid subject lines often used by spammers, online pornographers, and hackers:

Have you seen this one?

Hi Sweetie (or other term of endearment)

Are you ready for this?

Read this now!

Adults Only

An offer you can't refuse

Subject: URGENT!! VERY IMPORTANT!!! READ ME FIRST!!!

Labeling messages "Urgent" can be overdone. If something is really urgent, make a phone call.

Make the format fit the tone of your message.

The memo-like format of email makes salutations and closings optional in casual messages, but they're recommended in more formal messages or ones that are going to a foreign country.

Use a first name in the salutation only if you would use the person's first name when face-to-face. Make the formality of the closing match that of the salutation.

> Dear Professor Doerring:
> Very truly yours,
>
> Dear Analisa,
> Cordially,

Use the "cc:" or "bcc:" line.

When sending copies of a message to anyone other than the named recipient, use the "cc:" or "bcc:" line. The notation "cc:" in the heading stands for carbon copy; "bcc:" stands for blind carbon copy (terms that suggest their origins in the world of paper letters). If you want the recipient to know who is receiving a copy, put their names after "cc:"; if you don't want the names known, use the "bcc:" line.

> [S]ometimes we're curiously reluctant to let an old word do new tricks. We may talk about "electronic mail," for example, but we don't describe the online messages we receive as "electronic letters," maybe out of nostalgia for the smell of ink and paper.
> —Geoffrey Nunberg

Keep it short.

The revved-up atmosphere of email doesn't lend itself to lengthy discourse. Show that you're aware of demands on the recipient's time by being direct and concise.

> The editors of EEI Press present an interesting viewpoint in *E-What? A Guide to the Quirks of New Media Style and Usage* (EEI Press, 2000): A widely accepted statistic is that people read 25 percent slower on a computer screen than on paper. The corollary is that a document written for the Web should be 25 percent shorter than one written for print.

Use standard English.

English is a great way to express yourself. Though email encourages informality, a message is more understandable if it's written in complete sentences and uses words correctly. Acronyms unique to email, such as *btw* (by the way) and *lol* (laughing out loud), may not be familiar to your recipient. Emoticons and smiley faces are overly cute and may not transmit well on the Internet or translate well into other cultures.

That said, none of these considerations apply to casual exchanges when both parties are familiar with the lingo or to instant messaging, where speed rules.

Use uppercase and lowercase.

Don't write an entire message in capital letters. All caps is harder to read and is usually interpreted as shouting. For occasional emphasis, you can capitalize a word or phrase or surround it with asterisks. In general, however, when you have something important to say, let it be revealed by the words themselves, not by CAPS or a string of punctuation marks!!!!!

Keep line length short.

To avoid odd breaks that might happen with a long line of text, end the lines at about four inches (65–70 characters) by hitting "Enter." If you want to see how a message looks to the recipient, include your name on the mailing list or send yourself a bcc.

Use visual clues that transmit well on the Internet.

Numbered lists and short paragraphs capture attention and improve the chance that you will be understood. Skip the fancy stuff that works on the printed page but can come through as garbage on the screen (such as italics, boldface, em dashes). Any character that involves using the Control key is probably not going to transmit well.

Make replies clear.

Unless you're replying to a specific passage, put your response at the top of the message; the sender already knows what he or she said. But if you're replying to a specific point, insert your response directly below that point. Your response is easy to find if you start it with **** or <begin reply here>.

When replying to several points, put your response directly below each point. If there have been multiple exchanges of this sort, you create a document chain that allows you to follow the entire train of thought.

You're not through yet. Show one more touch of consideration by deleting the signature block of the original sender and any leftover pieces of incoming message that didn't require a response. This not only avoids confusion but saves scrolling time and memory.

Use a signature block where appropriate.

Close all business-related messages with a signature block. The signature block presents your full name and other pertinent information: your title, company name, phone and fax numbers, email address (include it as a courtesy, even though it also appears in the heading), and perhaps a web address. Remember to update the signature block in your email program if a component, such as the phone number, changes.

Limit the signature block to four or five lines. An added image or quotation will antagonize some recipients but please others, who find it helps convey an impression of you. Life's a gamble!

In personal messages use a signature block if you want to be sure the recipient has such information as phone or fax numbers. Otherwise, just close with a suitable sentiment (*Talk to you soon, Regards, Best, Ciao!*) and your name. Putting your name at the end of the message confirms that the message is complete.

Watch your language.

Watch your language when the recipient is in another country or from a different culture. I'm not referring to off-color or confrontational remarks (although it's a good idea to avoid them, too), but to idioms that don't translate well, such as

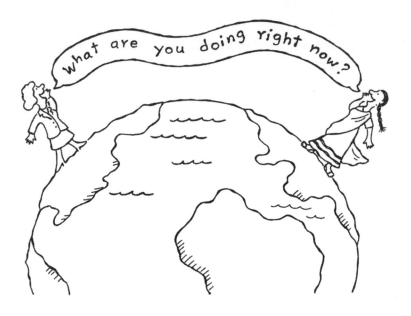

"pushing the envelope," "bite the bullet," and "connect the dots." Revise to avoid possible confusion.

Also watch for parochialisms, such as referring to the United States as "America" or its citizens as "Americans"—especially if the recipient lives in Canada, Chile, or any other North, Central, or South American country.

Proofread your email messages.

If a message is worth sending, it's worth proofing. Misspelled, omitted, or unintended words might send an entirely different message than the one you had in mind. While you're at it, check the address box (the "to:" line) to make sure the message is going to the correct person. If you were a bit careless when inserting a name from your address book—well, you can imagine the possibilities.

Be considerate about what you forward.

Common sense helps you decide which messages are suitable for forwarding. Here are my own preferences:

- CHAIN LETTERS: No. They are an imposition on the recipient and a waste of the Internet. I promise, you won't have bad luck by breaking the chain.

- PETITIONS: Maybe. Although they are generally ineffective and often a hoax, if they are about a subject of special concern to you, do it.

- JOKES: Yes, as long as they are welcome and don't contain anything that would be offensive to the recipients. Laughter heals.

- POLITICAL MESSAGES: Yes, to recipients you think would be interested. This aspect of email has turned the Internet into one of the most potent ways to mobilize grassroots sentiment.

Email provides so many advantages that it's worth chipping away at its drawbacks. As one Internet guru put it: Let's not turn the Information Superhighway into the Information Super Dump. We each have a role to play.

Appendix

Abbreviations

Two-Letter U.S. Commonwealth, District, State, and Territory Abbreviations

AK	Alaska	IL	Illinois
AL	Alabama	IN	Indiana
AR	Arkansas	KS	Kansas
AS	American Samoa	KY	Kentucky
AZ	Arizona	LA	Louisiana
CA	California	MA	Massachusetts
CO	Colorado	MD	Maryland
CT	Connecticut	ME	Maine
DC	District of Columbia	MI	Michigan
DE	Delaware	MN	Minnesota
FL	Florida	MO	Missouri
GA	Georgia	MS	Mississippi
GU	Guam	MT	Montana
HI	Hawaii	NC	North Carolina
IA	Iowa	ND	North Dakota
ID	Idaho	NE	Nebraska

NH	New Hampshire	SD	South Dakota
NJ	New Jersey	TN	Tennessee
NM	New Mexico	TX	Texas
NV	Nevada	UT	Utah
NY	New York	VA	Virginia
OH	Ohio	VI	Virgin Islands
OK	Oklahoma	VT	Vermont
OR	Oregon	WA	Washington
PA	Pennsylvania	WI	Wisconsin
PR	Puerto Rico	WV	West Virginia
RI	Rhode Island	WY	Wyoming
SC	South Carolina		

Two-Letter Canadian Province and Territory Abbreviations

AB	Alberta	NS	Nova Scotia
BC	British Columbia	ON	Ontario
LB	Labrador	PE	Prince Edward Island
MB	Manitoba	PQ	Quebec *or* Québec
NB	New Brunswick	SK	Saskatchewan
NF	Newfoundland	YT	Yukon Territories
NT	Northwest Territories *or* Nunavut		

Abbreviations Recommended by the U.S. Postal Service

Administration	Admn	Associate	Assoc
Agency	Agcy	Association	Assn
America	Amer	Attention	Attn
Apartment	Apt	Attorney	Atty

Avenue	Ave	Library	Lbry
Boulevard	Blvd	Management	Mgmt
Branch	Br	Manufacturing	Mfg
Bureau	Bur	Municipal	Mncpl
Center	Ctr	National	Natl
Circle	Cir	Office	Ofc
Commission	Comm	Organization	Orgn
Committee	Cmmte	Park	Park
Company	Co	Parkway	Pky
Comptroller	Comptlr	Place	Pl
Corporation	Corp	Plaza	Plz
Council	Cncl	Point	Pt
Court	Ct	Port	Prt
Department	Dept	Program	Prgm
Director	Dir	River	Riv
Drive	Dr	Road	Rd
Expressway	Expy	Secretary	Secy
Extension	Ext	Spring(s)	Spg(s)
Federal	Fed	Square	Sq
Financial	Fncl	Station	Sta
Government	Govt	Street	St
Highway	Hwy	Superintendent	Supt
Institute	Inst	Supervisor	Supvsr
International	Intrntl	System	Syst
Interstate	Intste	Terrace	Ter
Island	Is	Treasurer	Tres
Junction	Jct	Turnpike	Tpke
Laboratory	Lab	Valley	Vly
Lake	Lk	Village	Vlg
Landing	Lndg		

Forms of Address

Addressee	Address on Letter and Envelope	Salutation
PROFESSIONAL		
Attorney	[Full Name], Esq. [Local Address] or [Full Name], Attorney at law [Local Address]	Dear Mr./Ms. [Surname]:
Certified Public Accountant	[Full Name], CPA [Local Address]	Dear Mr./Ms. [Surname]:
Dentist	[Full Name], DDS (or DMD, etc.) or Dr. [Full Name] [Local Address]	Dear Dr. [Surname]:
Physician	[Full Name], MD or Dr. [Full Name] [Local Address]	Dear Dr. [Surname]:

Addressee	Address on Letter and Envelope	Salutation
Veterinarian	[Full Name], DVM or Dr. [Full Name] [Local Address]	Dear Dr. [Surname]:
GOVERNMENT		
The President	The President The White House Washington, DC 20500	Dear Mr./Madam President:
Spouse of the President	Mr./Mrs. [Surname] The White House Washington, DC 20500	Dear Mr./Mrs. [Surname]:
The Vice President	The Vice President United States Senate Washington, DC 20510 *or* The Honorable [Full Name] Vice President of the United States Washington, DC 20501	Dear Mr./Madam Vice President:

Addressee	Address on Letter and Envelope	Salutation
The Chief Justice	The Chief Justice of the United States The Supreme Court of the United States Washington, DC 20543	Dear Mr./Madam Chief Justice:
Associate Justice	Mr./Madam Justice [Surname] The Supreme Court of the United States Washington, DC 20543	Dear Mr./Madam Justice:
United States Senator	Honorable [Full Name] United States Senate Washington, DC 20515 or Honorable [Full Name] United States Senator [Local Address]	Dear Senator [Surname]:
United States Representative	Honorable [Full Name] House of Representatives Washington, DC 20515 or Honorable [Full Name] Member, United States House of Representatives [Local Address]	Dear Mr./Mrs./Ms. [Surname]:

Addressee	Address on Letter and Envelope	Salutation
Cabinet Members	Honorable [Full Name] Secretary of [Department Name] Washington, DC [zip code]	Dear Mr./Madam Secretary:
Ambassador, U.S.	Honorable [Full Name] The American Ambassador American Embassy [Local Address] [COUNTRY]	Dear Mr./Madam Ambassador:
Ambassador, Foreign	His/Her Excellency [Full Name] Ambassador of [Country] [Local Address]	Excellency: or Dear Mr./Mrs./Ms. Ambassador:
Governor	Honorable [Full Name] Governor of [State] State Capitol [Local Address]	Dear Governor [Surname]:

Addressee	Address on Letter and Envelope	Salutation
State Senator, Representative, Assemblyperson	Honorable [Full Name] [Local Address]	Dear Mr./Mrs./Ms. [Surname]:
Mayor	Honorable [Full Name] Mayor of [Name of City] City Hall [Local Address]	Dear Mayor [Surname]: or Dear Mr./Mrs./Ms. [Surname]:
Judge	Honorable [Full Name] [Name of Court] [Local Address]	Dear Judge [Surname]:
FOREIGN HEADS OF STATE Premier	His/Her Excellency [Full Name] Premier of [Country] [Local Address] [COUNTRY]	Dear Mr./Mrs./Ms. Premier:

Addressee	Address on Letter and Envelope	Salutation
President of a Republic	His/Her Excellency [Full Name] President of [Country] [Local Address] [COUNTRY]	Excellency: or Dear Mr./Madam President:
Prime Minister	His/Her Excellency [Full Name] [Local Address] [COUNTRY]	Excellency: or Dear Mr./Mrs./Ms. Prime Minister:
RELIGIOUS *Protestant*		
Episcopal Clergy	The Right Reverend [Full Name] Bishop of [Name] [Local Address] or The Very Reverend [Full Name] Dean of [Name] [Local Address]	Dear Bishop [Surname]: Dear Dean [Surname]:
Clergy with Doctor of Divinity Degree	The Reverend [Full Name], DD [Local Address]	Dear Dr. [Surname]: or Dear Reverend [Surname]:

Addressee	Address on Letter and Envelope	Salutation
Catholic		
The Pope	His Holiness, the Pope or His Holiness Pope [Name] Vatican City 00187 Rome ITALY	Your Holiness, or Most Holy Father,
		(complimentary close:) Your Holiness' most humble servant,
Cardinal	His Eminence [Given Name] Cardinal [Surname] Archbishop of [Diocese] [Local Address]	Your Eminence: (formal) or Dear Cardinal [Surname]: (less formal)
Bishop or Archbishop	The Most Reverend [Full Name] Bishop of [Diocese] or Archbishop of [Diocese] [Local Address]	Your Excellency: (formal) or Dear Archbishop [Surname]: (less formal)
Other Catholic Clergy	The Right Reverend Monsignor [Full Name] [Local Address]	Right Reverend Monsignor: (formal) or Dear Monsignor [Surname]: (less formal)

Addressee	Address on Letter and Envelope	Salutation
	The Reverend [Full Name and Initials of Order, if used] [Local Address]	Reverend Sir: (formal) or Dear Father [Surname]: (less formal)
	Mother [Full Name and Initials of Order, if used] [Local Address]	Dear Mother [Full Name]:
	Sister [Full Name and Initials of Order, if used] [Local Address]	Dear Sister [Full Name]:
Jewish		
With Academic Degree	Rabbi [Full Name] DD, LLD [Local Address]	Dear Rabbi [Surname]: or Dear Dr. [Surname]:
Without Academic Degree	Rabbi [Full Name] [Local Address]	Dear Rabbi [Surname]: or Dear Dr. [Surname]:
Muslim		
Imam	Imam [Full Name]	Dear Imam [Surname]:

Addressee	Address on Letter and Envelope	Salutation
SCHOOLS		
President of a College or University	Dr. [Full Name] President, [Name of Institution] [Local Address]	Dear Dr. [Surname]:
Dean	Dean [Full Name] School of [Name] [Name of Institution] [Local Address]	Dear Dean [Surname]:
Professor	Professor [Full Name] Department of [Name] [Name of Institution] [Local Address]	Dear Professor [Surname]:
MILITARY		
For Any Branch of Service	[Full or Abbreviated Rank] [Full Name], [Abbreviation of branch of service (USA, USAF, USCG, USMC, or USN)] [Military Address]	Dear [Full Rank] [Surname]:

Addressee	Address on Letter and Envelope	Salutation
U.S. Army, Air Force, and Marine Corps Personnel		
General	General [Full Name]	Dear General [Surname]:
Major General	Major General [Full Name]	Dear General [Surname]:
Lieutenant Colonel	Lieutenant Colonel [Full Name]	Dear Colonel [Surname]:
Captain	Captain [Full Name]	Dear Captain [Surname]:
Second Lieutenant	Second Lieutenant [Full Name]	Dear Lieutenant [Surname]:
Warrant Officer	Warrant Officer [Full Name]	Dear Mr./Ms. [Surname]:
Sergeant Major	Sergeant Major [Full Name]	Dear Sergeant Major [Surname]:
Master Sergeant	Master Sergeant [Full Name]	Dear Sergeant [Surname]:
Corporal	Corporal [Full Name]	Dear Corporal [Surname]:
Private First Class or Private	[Rank] [Full Name]	Dear Private [Surname]:
Airman First Class, Airman, or Basic Airman	[Rank] [Full Name]	Dear Airman [Surname]:

Addressee	Address on Letter and Envelope	Salutation
Navy Personnel		
Admiral	Admiral [Full Name]	Dear Admiral [Surname]:
Rear Admiral	Admiral [Full Name]	Dear Admiral [Surname]:
Captain	Captain [Full Name]	Dear Captain [Surname]:
Lieutenant Commander	Lieutenant Commander [Full Name]	Dear Commander [Surname]:
Lieutenant	Lieutenant [Full Name]	Dear Mr./Ms. [Surname]:
Ensign	Ensign [Full Name]	Dear Mr./Ms. [Surname]:
Warrant Officer (all grades)	Warrant Officer [Full Name]	Dear Mr./Ms. [Surname]:
Enlisted Personnel (all grades)	[Rank] [Full Name]	Dear Mr./Ms. [Surname]:
Retired	[Rank] [Full Name], [Abbreviation of service designation], Retired	Dear [Rank] [Surname]:

Internet Domain Names

U.S. Internet Domain Names

.com	U.S. commercial	.mil	U.S. Military
.edu	U.S. educational	.net	Network
.gov	U.S. Government	.org	Nonprofit Organization
.int	International		

Country-Code Top-Level Internet Domain Names

.ac	Ascension Island	.aq	Antarctica
.ad	Andorra	.ar	Argentina
.ae	United Arab Emirates	.as	American Samoa
.af	Afghanistan	.at	Austria
.ag	Antigua and Barbuda	.au	Australia
.ai	Anguilla	.aw	Aruba
.al	Albania	.az	Azerbaijan
.am	Armenia	.ba	Bosnia and Herzegovina
.an	Netherlands Antilles	.bb	Barbados
.ao	Angola	.bd	Bangladesh

.be	Belgium	.cr	Costa Rica
.bf	Burkina Faso	.cu	Cuba
.bg	Bulgaria	.cv	Cape Verde
.bh	Bahrain	.cx	Christmas Island
.bi	Burundi	.cy	Cyprus
.bj	Benin	.cz	Czech Republic
.bm	Bermuda	.de	Germany
.bn	Brunei Darussalam	.dj	Djibouti
.bo	Bolivia	.dk	Denmark
.br	Brazil	.dm	Dominica
.bs	Bahamas	.do	Dominican Republic
.bt	Bhutan	.dz	Algeria
.bv	Bouvet Island	.ec	Ecuador
.bw	Botswana	.ee	Estonia
.by	Belarus	.eg	Egypt
.bz	Belize	.eh	Western Sahara
.ca	Canada	.er	Eritrea
.cc	Cocos (Keeling) Islands	.es	Spain
		.et	Ethiopia
.cd	Congo, Democratic Republic of the	.eu	European Union
		.fi	Finland
.cf	Central African Republic	.fj	Fiji
		.fk	Falkland Islands (Malvinas)
.ch	Switzerland		
.ci	Côte D'Ivoire (Ivory Coast)	.fm	Micronesia
		.fo	Faroe Islands
.ck	Cook Islands	.fr	France
.cl	Chile	.fx	France, Metropolitan
.cm	Cameroon	.ga	Gabon
.cn	China	.gb	Great Britain (United Kingdom)
.co	Colombia		

.gd	Grenada	.io	British Indian Ocean Territory
.ge	Georgia	.iq	Iraq
.gf	French Guiana	.ir	Iran
.gg	Guernsey	.is	Iceland
.gh	Ghana	.it	Italy
.gi	Gibraltar	.je	Jersey
.gl	Greenland	.jm	Jamaica
.gm	Gambia	.jo	Jordan
.gn	Guinea	.jp	Japan
.gp	Guadeloupe	.ke	Kenya
.gq	Equatorial Guinea	.kg	Kyrgyzstan
.gr	Greece	.kh	Cambodia
.gs	South Georgia and South Sandwich Islands	.ki	Kiribati
		.km	Comoros
.gt	Guatemala	.kn	Saint Kitts and Nevis
.gu	Guam	.kp	Korea, Democratic People's Republic of (North)
.gw	Guinea-Bissau		
.gy	Guyana		
.hk	Hong Kong	.kr	Korea, Republic of (South)
.hm	Heard and McDonald Islands		
		.kw	Kuwait
.hn	Honduras	.ky	Cayman Islands
.hr	Croatia (Hrvatska)	.kz	Kazakhstan
.ht	Haiti	.la	Laos
.hu	Hungary	.lb	Lebanon
.id	Indonesia	.lc	Saint Lucia
.ie	Ireland	.li	Liechtenstein
.il	Israel	.lk	Sri Lanka
.im	Isle of Man	.lr	Liberia
.in	India	.ls	Lesotho

.lt	Lithuania	.ni	Nicaragua
.lu	Luxembourg	.nl	Netherlands
.lv	Latvia	.no	Norway
.ly	Libya	.np	Nepal
.ma	Morocco	.nr	Nauru
.mc	Monaco	.nt	Neutral Zone
.md	Moldova	.nu	Niue
.mg	Madagascar	.nz	New Zealand
.mh	Marshall Islands		(Aotearoa)
.mk	Macedonia	.om	Oman
.ml	Mali	.pa	Panama
.mm	Myanmar	.pe	Peru
.mn	Mongolia	.pf	French Polynesia
.mo	Macau	.pg	Papua New Guinea
.mp	Northern Mariana	.ph	Philippines
	Islands	.pk	Pakistan
.mq	Martinique	.pl	Poland
.mr	Mauritania	.pm	St.-Pierre and Miquelon
.ms	Montserrat	.pn	Pitcairn
.mt	Malta	.pr	Puerto Rico
.mu	Mauritius	.pt	Portugal
.mv	Maldives	.pw	Palau
.mw	Malawi	.py	Paraguay
.mx	Mexico	.qa	Qatar
.my	Malaysia	.re	Reunion
.mz	Mozambique	.ro	Romania
.na	Namibia	.ru	Russian Federation
.nc	New Caledonia	.rw	Rwanda
.ne	Niger	.sa	Saudi Arabia
.nf	Norfolk Island	.sb	Solomon Islands
.ng	Nigeria	.sc	Seychelles

.sd	Sudan	.tp	East Timor
.se	Sweden	.tr	Turkey
.sg	Singapore	.tt	Trinidad and Tobago
.sh	St. Helena	.tv	Tuvalu
.si	Slovenia	.tw	Taiwan
.sj	Svalbard and Jan Mayen Islands	.tz	Tanzania
		.ua	Ukraine
.sk	Slovak Republic	.ug	Uganda
.sl	Sierra Leone	.uk	United Kingdom
.sm	San Marino	.um	U.S. Minor Outlying Islands
.sn	Senegal		
.so	Somalia	.us	United States
.sr	Suriname	.uy	Uruguay
.st	São Tomé and Príncipe	.uz	Uzbekistan
		.va	Holy See (Vatican City State)
.su	USSR (former)		
.sv	El Salvador	.vc	Saint Vincent and the Grenadines
.sy	Syria		
.sz	Swaziland	.ve	Venezuela
.tc	Turks and Caicos Islands	.vg	Virgin Islands (British)
		.vi	Virgin Islands (U.S.)
.td	Chad	.vn	Vietnam
.tf	French Southern Territories	.vu	Vanuatu
		.wf	Wallis and Futuna
.tg	Togo	.ws	Samoa
.th	Thailand	.ye	Yemen
.tj	Tajikistan	.yt	Mayotte
.tk	Tokelau	.yu	Yugoslavia
.tm	Turkmenistan	.za	South Africa
.tn	Tunisia	.zm	Zambia
.to	Tonga	.zw	Zimbabwe

Index

140